Adirondack Portraits

A York State Book

ADIRONDACK

Edited by

NOEL RIEDINGER-JOHNSON

PORTRAITS

A Piece of Time

JEANNE ROBERT FOSTER

Foreword by
ALFRED KAZIN   *SYRACUSE UNIVERSITY PRESS*   *1986*

First Edition, 1986

15 16 17 18 19 20   9 8 7 6 5 4

Drawing, page i: "Road to Crane Mountain," by Grace Oehser. Reprinted with permission. Brush-and-ink sketches by Grace Oehser introducing the four sections of poetry in *Adirondack Portraits* used by the permission of the artist.

∞ The paper used in this publication meets the minimum requirements of the American National Standard for Information Sciences—Permanence of Paper for Printed Library Materials, ANSI Z39.48-1992.

For a listing of books published and distributed by Syracuse University Press, visit https://press.syr.edu.

ISBN: 978-0-8156-0205-7 (paper)

Library of Congress Cataloging-in-Publication Data

Foster, Jeanne Robert, 1879–1970.
    Adirondack portraits.

    (A York State book)
    Includes index.
    1. Adirondack Mountains (N.Y.)—Literary collections.
2. Foster, Jeanne Robert, 1879–1970—Biography.
3. Authors, American—20th century—Biography.
4. Adirondack Mountains (N.Y.)—Social life and customs.
I. Riedinger-Johnson, Noel. II. Title.
PS3511.0689A67 1986   811'.52   86-6044
ISBN 0-8156-2377-1 (alk. paper)
ISBN 0-8156-0205-7 (pbk. : alk. paper)

Manufactured in the United States of America

Dedicated to Paul Schaefer

Shepherd of the Wilderness

I salute you,
Preserver of the Wilderness,
Keeper of the waters—
Of the lakes, rivers and hidden sources,
Of the soil and the crested ranges,
The intervales and the high peaks,
The wild beauty, the vanishing life
Of the deep forests,
Of our magnificent heritage. . .
I salute you.

I, who in the shadow of Marcy
In childhood, saw Whiteface shine
Tipped with the sunrise,
Who knew the life of old lumbercamps
And the shanty roads,
Who loved the "Indian Pipe" in the shadow
Of the firs and the bright azaleas
Upon the swamplands,
I salute you.

You, who watch the flight of the eagle
And hark the cry of the loon,
Aware that in the wilderness,
The spirit of man
Alone finds strength and renewal,
Your fellow men salute you.

Other Works by Jeanne Robert Foster

Wild Apples, Sherman, French and Company, Boston, 1916

Neighbors of Yesterday, Sherman, French and Company, Boston, 1916; reprinted, Riedinger and Riedinger Limited, Schenectady, N.Y., 1963

Rock Flower, Boni and Liveright, New York, 1922

The John Quinn Letters (ed.), New York Public Library, 1925

Awakening Grace (ed. Jeanne and Darwin Shaw), Sherlar Press, North Myrtle Beach, S.C., 1977

CONTENTS

FOREWORD

I HAD NEVER heard of Jeanne Robert Foster when Noel Riedinger-Johnson placed this book in my hands. Turning its pages, not at all sure what to expect, I became aware of an extraordinary woman—an almost classic American story of personal migration from the nineteenth century to the twentieth—and the most deeply felt literary portrait I had ever encountered, about a region that still seems remote and strange even to other New Yorkers—the great Adirondack Forest Preserve kept "forever wild" by the authority of the State of New York.

Nothing is so common and traditional in American annals as the story of a gifted person from a "lowly," even primitive, background who becomes a shining example of self discovery and makes it to the great world. But there is something still astonishing and almost unreal in Jeanne Robert Foster's move from the isolated North Woods country in which she was born in 1879 to the New York of the Armory Show, John Butler Yeats, the Irish-American lawyer and art patron John Quinn, the Paris in the 1920s of Picasso, Joyce, Pound.

Jeanne was strikingly attractive, a sometime model for illustrators and painters, equally vivid in thought and speech. Having expected little enough coming from a family so poor that she was often farmed out so there would be one less mouth to feed, she must have seemed all the more eager and interesting when she encountered in New York's Chelsea such a fabulously influential personality as the painter John Butler Yeats. Old Yeats in New York before World War I used to say that he was there because Ireland was too small to hold him and his famous son "Willie." There is a wonderful painting by John Sloan of a group in Petipas' Restaurant on West 23rd Street that John Butler Yeats made his favorite hangout. The painting shows some very interesting people—among them the young Van Wyck Brooks. For all I know, Jeanne Robert Foster is in the painting. But what is most striking about it is the gleam, the charm, the unforgettable vivacity of John Butler Yeats's face. The famous quality of his talk and his merry, almost rakishly paternal benevolence to young writers and artists of the "little renaissance" in pre-war New York can still be felt over the years. Jeanne was lucky to know him—and he was understandably responsive to her glowing presence.

Her great friend John Quinn was a rather more severe type. But he was like a Renaissance Pope or Florentine prince in his eager patronage of modern literature and art. Quinn did more to advance the fortunes of James Joyce than anyone except his British patron Harriet Weaver. To a literary critic and literary historian like myself, who has spent much of his life pursuing the great twentieth-century thinkers and modernists, it is thrilling to read of Jeanne Robert Foster's encounters with William James and George Santayana at Harvard. As co-worker with and agent for Quinn when he was assembling his collection of contemporary art, she came to know Pablo Picasso, Constantin Brancusi, André Derain, Gwen John. I was particularly fascinated to learn of her participation in the *Transatlantic Review,* edited by Ford Madox Ford. Hemingway's early pieces appeared there, and she also helped Ford with editing chores. Of course no figure of the time was more influential than Ezra Pound when he was promoting what he grandly called the "American Risorgimento"; Jeanne served Pound for a time as his American agent.

Yet the really extraordinary thing about Jeanne Robert Foster's move into this brilliantly cosmopolitan art world in London, Paris, New York, is that in her own mind she never really left the Adirondack Country. In memory and imagination she increasingly pondered and cherished the rough surroundings and deeply isolated people that were her first and enduring background in life.

Jeanne Robert Foster confronted these images in her mind both in prose and verse. The verse is particularly striking in its matter-of-fact plainness. I do not know if she particularly cared for Robert Frost, but the poems in this book serve more than the prose sketches for the recovery of a "piece of time," and they are an astonishing duplicate of Frost's slow-moving, artfully conversational pastorals.

It would be interesting to know if someone who was friendly with Eliot and Pound was actually more indebted to the poems of Robert Frost. Perhaps she simply fell into a form so appropriate to "country things" because of the materials so personal to her. The slow pace of talk, the tide of memories, the prevailing theme of nature as adversary seem very familiar, and haunting, when we read in Jeanne Robert Foster of farms where there was often more stone than soil, and where there were less than a hundred frost-free days a year.

Robert Frost was, of course, a master poet for whom each poem was what he proudly called an example of "prowess." Jeanne Robert Foster was less interested in poetry than in the world it could report. Nor could she have duplicated Frost's own bitter determination as he took on all nature as a personal challenge. To have great poets you must have great egos. That was not her style. But one of her best poems, "Jen Murdock's Roosters," begins with a line that is pure Robert Frost—"Nature don't listen to us very much"; it goes on "When we tell her what to do, she veers off/ On some road she had in her mind/ Before we were born."

No, Jeanne Robert Foster was not interested in poetry for poetry's sake. This book is exactly what the title says it is: "a piece of time." It is above all an attempt to recover a vanished time, to record with love, admiration and enduring wonder a life of hardship, endless exertion, and, perhaps above all, the kind of isolation that used to dominate country life in America—nowhere more than in the Adirondacks. More than anything else, the book is an attempt to picture in tones often sorrowful yet wry a world—the North Woods life at the end of the nineteenth century—that to this day remains a "last frontier."

The Adirondacks two hundred and fifty miles north of New York had still no record of being traversed long after Lewis and Clark had reached the Pacific Coast. To this day, "forever wild" and protected in its necessary wildness by express mandate in the New York State Constitution, it seems to the vacationer, hiker, or occasional hunter more a place for recreation than one where families live and have lived for more than a century. Yet when Jeanne Robert Foster grew up there, moving about in her father's search for a living, what was most striking to her was that it was "home"— and not only sacred as such, but also of extraordinary interest to someone meant to become a writer.

Among other things, the Adirondacks in their vastness and even their fearsomeness answered to the land hunger that drove so many impoverished Europeans from famine and conscription and family divisions to the New World. One of the most gripping details in the book is the story of the Irish family that fled famine to this remote region. They remained so anxious about this one plot of land they felt privileged to acquire that they would not leave it even on Sundays to attend mass. A priest had from time to time to come to them.

"We were the only American family," Jeanne Robert Foster says at one point, remembering the Christmases of her youth, "the only family with early American ancestors in the little farming settlement of houses. The others were French (France-French) and Canadians (Canadian-French) and Protestant Irish from the North of Ireland." Like her contemporary, Willa Cather in Nebraska, who developed a passion for older cultures from living among Bohemian farmers, Jeanne Foster's instinct developed early—right where she grew up—for the more cosmopolitan world she was to know. She demonstrates page after page a gift for entering into the lives of other people, for sharing imaginatively their poverty, their isolation, even their eccentricity.

I am not likely soon to forget "Old Man Wamsley" ("I never knew that he had a first name"). He lived on the windy hill that looked up to Mount Marcy and White-face Mountain. He was stiff, unbending, savage of temper. His house had no furnishings, blinds, curtains; just the bare floor, a sheet-iron stove, a few wooden chairs.

> When the neighborhood women offered to make curtains
> Before his wife faded away from her hard life,
> He refused. "Windows are to let in the light.
> I don't want lace hung there to dull the light.
> And I want to look out on whatever's around."

"The old man would come out roaring at me" when he saw Jeanne with her small tin pail coming anywhere near the largest Seckel pear tree she had ever seen. "What did I think, that he would give away his pears?" But as she turned to go down the hill, "always the gate would open/ And the old man would pull me into the orchard,/ And still growling, fill my small pail."

In that often abrasive environment, the damage that could be inflicted on people's souls is most vividly presented in the story of the man confined in a room "who danced himself to death." A particularly haunting poem this, "The Dancing Man," full of the ghosts and supernatural lore that once filled up the great silences that prevailed in remote country districts. Hezzie Daly one Sunday heard a sermon "On King

David dancing before the Ark." "Hezzie started dancing on the way home/ And never stopped as long as he had life./ He hardly slept; nothing could quiet him;/ He said he was praising God by dancing."

Growing up so much a part of "country things," Jeanne Foster could never forget the heady combination of rivers, forests, and mountains that made the Adirondacks unique. The woman who was to know Picasso and Pound in the Paris of the 1920s had never seen telegraph wires until her father, driving a farm wagon, first pointed them out to her. Nor could she ever forget the twelve-hour days worked by the loggers, or the children from families so impoverished that they went barefoot in zero weather. The father declared that they would not be "beholden" to the "poormaster."

When photography reached the Adirondacks in the 1880s (the photographs preserved from the earliest period are a striking feature of this book), two brothers preparing to pose disclosed that they had just one "boiled shirt" between them and took turns wearing it. There are wonderful touches throughout the book that bring back that now remote period in that still "leftover" region—the stiff and stilted "best rooms" into which no one entered except on the most awesome occasions; the minister who regularly preached hell and damnation but was so affected by the hard times afflicting his congregation that he was prepared to forego the usual harshness of his sermon; the horse kept by a farmer so poor and grim that the horse fed himself by seizing the apples from the lowest branches. Throughout the book one is aware of a life long gone, gone, gone. But dominating all is Jeanne Robert Foster's loving voice. In the poem "Griffin" she remembers "There was a waitress lovely as a fawn/ And shy as one, who served the pork and beans./ She looked like china when the light shines through."

When that charming writer E. B. White moved from New York City to remote Maine, he explained that he was more than tired of the crammed disorderly urban scene and was "homesick for loneliness." That is the quintessential note of an "old time America" that made the rapture-in-landscape that fills the writings of Henry David Thoreau, John Muir, and many other "early table Americans." Jeanne Robert Foster is one of them. The book is a thoroughly unexpected, delightful contribution to our living. It fills a void left in our hearts by the demons of progress and the acceleration of time.

Alfred Kazin

New York City
January 1986

xiv

PREFACE

THE STORIES of my old neighbors and friends that come to you are true stories of real persons who lived in the North Woods before the turn of the century. They were natives of three counties—Essex, Warren, and Hamilton—and, in the main, descendants of the original settlers. They speak to you exactly as they spoke long ago. Neither their speech nor their stories have been altered, nor their portraits retouched.

If you travel through the Adirondack wilderness now on the new roads, you will not find people like these old neighbors and lumberjacks, for the breed is gone. You may find, on one of the dirt side roads, signs of where an old log house once stood. There may be, on what seems to be wild land, a tangle of crab-apple trees, lilacs mixed with the brush, or a stray clump of dark-blue columbine.

If you follow what was once a "tote road" into the deep woods, you will come upon moss-covered logs that were once part of the foundation of a lumber shanty. And in a backwater of life in the region, you can still find a very aged person who remembers the old lumbering days and perhaps hear a verse or two of an authentic shanty song that was handed down orally.

But for the most part the life of farmers and lumbermen one hundred years ago is lost and forgotten. Hemlock bark is no longer peeled from the trees and shipped to the tanneries, for they are gone, and wherever lumbering is done today the power saw has replaced the shanty chopper's double-bitted ax.

In the farm houses you will no longer find the rag-carpet looms or the spinning wheels; and the farmers cannot open a barn door to show a fanning mill for buckwheat or a horse-power threshing machine for oats. Together with much else that was useful and beautiful, they belong to yesterday, to a way of life that has vanished, never to return. To bring you pictures of these kindly neighbors and lumberjacks, also neighbors, I have set down these stories, memories that still fill my mind in a thrilling and unforgettable procession.

Jeanne Robert Foster

ACKNOWLEDGMENTS

THE MAIN SELECTION of poetry, prose, and photographs of this manuscript is part of the Jeanne Robert Foster Collection of Albert A. ("Tex") Riedinger and Ruth Riedinger. Their interest in the Adirondacks and their extensive efforts in reprinting and distributing *Neighbors of Yesterday* in the early 1960s encouraged Jeanne to believe that her unpublished Adirondack poetry and prose would find its way to the public in a form that would help preserve some of the cultural history of the region. The collection, which also includes photographs, letters, lecture notes, books, scrapbooks, and art work, is now in the possession of Theodore A. Riedinger and Noel Riedinger-Johnson. (The biographical information included has been drawn primarily from Jeanne's extensive correspondence with a wide range of individuals.)

Special recognition must be given to Paul Schaefer, the noted New York State conservationist (and recipient of an honorary doctorate from Union College for his conservation work), who became a close friend of Jeanne. He granted complete access to and use of his letters, photographs, articles, and other materials. Without his sensitive insight and understanding of the Adirondacks and their importance to Jeanne, this book would not have been possible.

Richard Londraville, professor of English at the State University of New York at Potsdam, opened his collection and granted permission to use information from his unfinished and unpublished biography of Jeanne Robert Foster. It should be noted that he has written and published several informative articles about Jeanne.

Warder Cadbury, professor of philosophy at the State University of New York at Albany, shared his many letters from Jeanne. She appreciated his expertise in Adirondack art and literature, and his work with the Adirondack Museum during the early stages of its development.

Myrtle Putnam Buyce, granddaughter of O. D. Putnam; Adeline Armstrong O'Byrne, granddaughter of Enos O. Putnam; and Adorna Wright, grand-niece of Frank Oliver, shared many family letters and memories.

Additional information was obtained from the records of the historical societies in the towns of Minerva, Chestertown, and Thurman, New York; the Adirondack Museum; the John Quinn Memorial Collection, the Yeats-Foster-Quinn Collection, and the Jeanne Robert Foster–William M. Murphy Collection in the Rare Books and

Manuscripts Division (Astor, Lenox and Tilden foundations), at the New York Public Library; the Aline Saarinen Papers in the Archives of American Art at the Smithsonian Institution, Washington; the Judith Zilczer Papers in the archives of the Smithsonian Institution; and the files of Robert Doty, director of the Currier Gallery of Art.

Special thanks go to the following individuals who gave unselfishly of themselves to help complete this book. Ann Wait spent months reviewing and organizing the Jeanne Robert Foster Collection, and cataloged and printed the Putnam glass-plate negatives which are an important part of the collection. Catherine Clarke, a gifted poet in her own right, initially edited the poems. The majority existed in at least two and sometimes as many as five or six versions. Editing them consisted of a close and careful comparison of each variant to select the word, line, or stanza from several possibilities that would work best in the finished poem. Catherine Clarke's concern throughout was to preserve Jeanne Robert Foster's original structures and sequences.

Paul H. Oehser contributed his extensive editorial expertise and guidance throughout the development of the manuscript, and completed the final editing of the book. Former director of the Smithsonian Institution Press and, upon retirement, editor of the research reports for the National Geographic Society, he has published several books, including *Fifty Poems, The Witch of Scrapfaggot Green,* and three books on the history, organization, and activities of the Smithsonian Institution.

Grace Oehser lent her pen-and-ink drawing of the Putnam farmhouse that she drew in 1959, before the house was torn down. She also executed four brush-and-ink drawings of places that had been important to Jeanne. (Mrs. Oehser has exhibited in the Washington, D.C., area and at the Adirondack Museum.)

Alfred Kazin, distinguished literary critic and professor at the Graduate School and University Center of the City University of New York, evaluated Jeanne's poetry and prose and encouraged the publication of her work. His latest book, *An American Procession,* explores the relationship between American history and literature.

Michael Gladstone, director of the Publishing Center for Cultural Resources, helped to clarify the relationship between the author, editor, and reader by suggesting a better combination of the diverse elements in the book.

Ben L. Reid, retired chairman of the English Department at Mount Holyoke College, shared the knowledge he gained while working with Jeanne in the preparation of his biography, *Man from New York: John Quinn and His Friends,* which won the Pulitzer Prize in 1969.

Judith Zilczer, research historian at the Hirshhorn Museum and Sculpture Garden of the Smithsonian Institution, provided a new perspective of Jeanne's contribution to the avant-garde—a perspective she gained during her research for her monograph, *"The Noble Buyer": John Quinn, Patron of the Avant-Garde,* which was prepared in conjunction with the memorial exhibition of Quinn's art collection.

Lewis Waddell, historian for the Town of Johnsburg; Mabel Jones, historian for the Town of Minerva; Thomas and Jane Parrott, historians for the Town of Chester; and Ted Aber, historian for both the Town of Indian Lake and Hamilton County, carefully read the manuscript and reviewed the photographs for historical accuracy, and provided invaluable information about Johnsburg, Minerva, Chestertown, and Blue Mountain Lake. They were a mine of information about the Oliver and Putnam families and their relatives, and verified information about the people and places in the poems and prose. Myra Magee, former historian for the Town of Thurman, and

Pamela Vogel, historian for Warren County, provided additional information. Thomas Magee of Chestertown generously lent his original 1876 maps of Johnsburg, Minerva, and Chestertown for reproduction.

Hugh Flick, retired associate commissioner for cultural education for the New York State Department of Education and president of the New York State Historical Association, reviewed the manuscript. His comments on the selective use of historical data in order to add dimension to Jeanne's poetry and prose were extremely helpful.

Clint and Mary Whittemore read the poetry and prose for authenticity, drawing on their early life in the Adirondacks. A writer, Mary Whittemore is the great-granddaughter of "Old Man Wamsley" and was raised in Minerva. With Mabel Jones, Mary guided a tour of Jeanne's "Neighborhood" in Minerva, which included the log cabin where her grandmother was born.

Alice Gilborn emphasized the importance of Jeanne's contribution to Adirondack literature and encouraged publication. She is the editor of *Blueline,* the literary publication of the Adirondacks, and has written two informative articles on Jeanne's poetry.

Annette Kolodny, professor of literature at Rensselaer Polytechnic Institute, Judith Fetterley, associate professor of English at the State University of New York at Albany, and Kate Winter, lecturer in the English Department at the State University of New York at Albany, all specializing in women's literature, discussed the manuscript and the current focus on early women writers.

Ann Seemann, librarian of Schaffer Library, Union College, opened the doors of her library, provided research assistance, and encouraged long hours of careful study. Ellen Fladger, library archivist and a specialist on glass-plate negatives was a valuable consultant on the printing of the Putman photographs.

Paul Schaefer, Norman VanValkenburgh, Warder Cadbury, Philip Terrie, Lisa Westervelt, Betty Price, and Robert DeYoung carefully read the manuscript and offered cogent criticisms and suggestions. William Dunham, David Beim, Drayton Grant, Annette Kolodny, and Kate Winter recommended approaches to publishers.

Darwin Shaw, a close friend of Jeanne's, contributed a valuable insight into Jeanne's religious and philosophical thoughts in the course of several lengthy discussions. He and his wife Jeanne edited and published *Awakening Grace* in 1977, a collection of Jeanne's spiritual poetry.

Joseph Mosarra, retired executive director of the Schenectady Senior Citizens' Center, recalled his rewarding years working with Jeanne and shared his letters.

Betsy McCamic Tisdale and Lillian Barden spent hours typing and proof-reading the manuscript. Both offered careful and helpful observations as work on the typescript progressed.

Without the help of these individuals, and of others too numerous to list, and without the encouragement and support of Dan Johnson and John Clarke, who lived with the dreams and the heartaches of the long months of researching, editing, and writing, this book could never have become a reality.

Noel Riedinger-Johnson

Schenectady, N.Y.
Spring 1986

Jeanne Robert Foster

JEANNE ROBERT FOSTER

1879–1970

EANNE ROBERT FOSTER came of age as the United States was entering a new century. The quiet agrarian nation was turning into a vibrant industrialized giant, with brash new cities that rivaled those of Europe. New York, with more than a million people, was the largest and most sophisticated city in the nation—and the third largest in the world.

Yet, two hundred and fifty miles north of New York City, loomed the inhospitable Adirondacks—a vast mountainous region that still had no record of being traversed decades after Lewis and Clark had crossed the Rocky Mountains to reach the Pacific Coast. On state maps it was referred to as the "Adirondack Wilderness" or the "Great Forest." Some knew it as a playground of the rich, where the wealthy vacationed at the shores of crystal lakes or followed hired guides on hunting or fishing excursions. Few outsiders knew of the lumberjacks and farmers in isolated Adirondack communities who scraped a living out of the mountains' rough terrain. There had never been a mass migration into this frontier—no wagon trains, no cowboys, few, if any, Indians, no offers of free land, no easy promise of the good life just over the next ridge. Most of the pioneers had moved on to the fertile lowlands to the west via the St. Lawrence River on the north or the Erie Canal on the south; only a few hardy settlers ventured into the mountains—and fewer yet stayed on. The Adirondacks were, in short, America's last frontier.

Jeanne Robert Foster was born in these mountains in the small town of Johnsburg in 1879, the first child of Frank and Lizzy Oliver, a lumberjack and a school teacher. They named her Julia Elizabeth Oliver; Jeanne Robert Foster was the penname she used after her marriage to Matlock Foster in 1896. Her early life was much like that of her parents and grandparents—a struggle against nature's odds to stay alive. Yet her early years in the mountains prepared her for the entirely different life she would seek—and find—in New York only a few short years later, where she would earn a degree of recognition remarkable for a woman of that day.

Jeanne's family was impoverished. Her father worked the forests and fields of the mountains as his father had done before him. He was a soft-spoken, deeply religious man, whose compassion for people and love for the land would take root in his precocious daughter.[1] His quiet manner was in sharp contrast to Jeanne's mother, who had been raised in the family of a fiery abolitionist minister dedicated to the fight for equality and human dignity for all people.[2] She was a determined woman, a college graduate who had taught outside of the Adirondacks before she returned to the mountains to marry Jeanne's father. She recognized the importance of education and pressed her daughter to study, to use her mind, and to look beyond the Adirondacks to a country in the midst of rapid growth, a country where exciting new avenues were opening up for women.[3]

Life in Jeanne's family was tenuous, for it was not easy to live in the mountains' relentless and unforgiving environment. While there was ample wood and water, the rugged terrain and thin soil made it difficult to raise enough food to last through the long, cold, snow-bound winters. Sickness and disease were common, and a simple error in judgment could mean disaster or even death. Jeanne shared in her family's

Matt Foster (*left*) with his brother on the Putnam farm in the Adirondacks, c. 1896. Photographer unknown.

struggle for survival. In addition, as the oldest and strongest and most intelligent of the children, she often acted as the buffer between her very different parents. She was the one who did the farm chores when her father was in lumber camp for months on end in winter, who cared for the sick, and walked miles alone through the forests to fetch the mail, who was farmed out to relatives when there wasn't enough to go around, and who guided tourists up the mountain to earn a little money to help her parents.

Yet Jeanne did not dwell on the hardships. She quickly learned of the self-renewal of nature and of the sustaining strength of the mountains.[4] She became sensitive to others and to the human condition generally, since existence in the mountains depended on mutual cooperation and understanding. She found in the love and support of her extended family the encouragement she needed to seek new horizons and to break new ground. The pioneering spirit of her family was in her blood, and she was ready to be a part of a young country that was in the process of developing its own identity. In her long life, Jeanne was to help open frontiers of literature, art, and social reform in her country.

At fifteen, Jeanne was teaching in small North Country schools, living either with relatives or with her students' families.[5] Economic pressures forced her parents to move to the southern edge of the Adirondacks in 1896. The country was still reeling from the financial collapse of 1893, and the lumber industry in the Adirondacks was under serious attack from another quarter. In 1885, New York State had established the New York State Forest Preserve, consisting of state lands in both the Adirondack and Catskill Mountains. Its intent was to protect the state's watershed resources from the continued threat of extensive lumbering and the resulting forest fires that swept over the mountains. In 1894 the state electorate had added the now famous "Forever Wild" covenant to the New York State Constitution, providing iron-clad protection to the state's forests.

For many, however, like Jeanne's father, the mountains could no longer provide even a meager economic base. In 1896, Frank Oliver moved his wife and part of his family to Glens Falls, where he went to work as a carpenter at the Glens Falls Opera House. Jeanne's mother was delighted to be in a city that offered at least some cultural advantages, and she encouraged Jeanne to join them and study French and music.[6] But Jeanne never reached Glens Falls: that summer, at age seventeen, she married Matlock Foster, a man twenty-five years her senior. An insurance agent from Rochester, he was the son of her family's next-door neighbor in Chestertown. She left the Adirondacks the young wife of an established gentleman who apparently recognized not only his wife's beauty and intelligence but also her expanding cultural interests as well. For the next eleven years she moved between Rochester and New York City to care for her aging mother-in-law, who died in 1904, and her brother-in-law, Gardiner Foster, an ophthalmologist.[7] Her marriage gave her the social position and respectability that she would find so important later on. Much more significantly, it gave her the chance to move to the city that was the very pulse of a changing America.

Jeanne's life in Rochester and New York City contrasted sharply with that of the isolated Adirondack communities of her youth and young womanhood. She moved from a bleak existence of log structures and calico pinafores into the glittering world of Victorian opulence. With the opulence, however, came the Victorian perception that women belonged at home caring for husbands and children. They did not belong in business or in the professions. They did not need higher education, since there was no need for them to make decisions. They had few rights and could not vote. Jeanne

Jeanne Robert Foster at the Putnam farm about the time of her marriage, c. 1896.
Photographer unknown.

could not accept these attitudes that were so different from the stark realities of the
Adirondacks, where women worked side by side with men in their daily struggle with
the elements. In her family, Jeanne had been her father's strong "son" as well as her
mother's sensitive daughter. Alongside her father she had cared for the livestock,
handled the farm chores, helped in the fields, and even skidded logs in the forest. With
her mother she had tended the garden, "put by" the produce, cooked and cleaned, and
cared for the younger children, the sick, and the elderly. For her, there could never be a
clearly defined—and plainly subordinate—role for women. Just as necessity had man-
dated that she roam the mountains, dense forests, and lakes and rivers of the Adiron-
dacks (then considered a decidedly "masculine domain"), she chose to go beyond the
Victorian constraints imposed on the women of her day. Without the responsibility of
children—Jeanne lost her only child, stillborn, during the first year of her marriage[8]—

she had the freedom to explore areas that were still traditionally dominated by men.

Jeanne's husband encouraged his young wife.[9] In the early years of their marriage Jeanne graduated from the Rochester Athenaeum and Mechanics Institute in Rochester and from the Stanhope-Wheatcroft Dramatic School in New York. Acting was one of the few professions that included women, and Jeanne became an ingenue with the American Stock Company, where she played some secondary roles under the stage name of Jean Elspeth. She also assisted Grace Margaret Gould, fashion editor of the Hearst papers, with the design of the fashion pages for the *New York Sunday American*. The paper employed a number of beautiful models, who were photographed weekly in the latest fashions of the day. Gould asked Jeanne if she would be willing to model as well as to assist with the mechanics of page layout. Jeanne agreed and parlayed this experience into a flourishing career after joining the Model's Club. She appeared on the cover of *Vanity Fair*, and posed for some of the leading illustrators in the country: Charles Dana Gibson, Philip Boileau, Albert Wenzell, and Harrison Fisher.[10] She became Fisher's leading model as the "Fisher Girl," and drawings of her appeared in newspapers, magazines, and books.[11]

Jeanne's work with illustrators gave her an appreciation for art, and she began to visit the New York galleries. She felt the excitement that prevailed in that city at the turn of the century, yet she was ever conscious of the provinciality that typified so much of Victorian America.[12] Most of her earnings she sent back to her struggling family, whom she had established in a house on the outskirts of Schenectady that Jeanne had purchased in 1901.[13]

Sometime around 1907[14] one of Jeanne's sisters became seriously ill, and

The two distinct faces of Jeanne Robert Foster are nicely caught in this pen and ink drawing by a staff artist at *Vanity Fair*, 1902.

Harrison Fisher's drawings of Jeanne appeared across the United States and in Europe. Jeanne found this postcard in England.

Jeanne left New York for Boston to care for her. She and her husband decided to move there, and stayed on for about three years. Jeanne enjoyed Boston's cultural atmosphere—the museums, the galleries, Isabella Stewart Gardner's art collection— as well as horseback riding on the Fenway. She attended Boston University and took extension courses at Harvard, studying philosophy under the likes of William James, George Palmer, Josiah Royce, and George Santayana.[15] She took composition with Charles Townsend Copeland. Her professors must have appreciated the intensity of their student, now nearing thirty years of age, in whom the more observant must have seen not only an unusual eagerness for knowledge but also almost the personification of turn-of-the-century America in transition. She was fortunate to have lived in the Adirondacks, where she had had to deal with fundamental questions of life and death and the curious interrelationship of man and nature. She had then taken the bold step of moving to New York City, where she confronted a much more sophisticated life, but one based on comparatively superficial values. Here, as a model, she had used her beauty, but in a way very much her own. Whereas women were generally presented by artists in an idealized form to represent beauty, purity, and the tenderness of motherhood—values in sharp contrast to the impersonal mechanized business world of men—Jeanne was able to move from modeling into journalism, a field that accepted women in its professional ranks but was still very much controlled by men. Now, in Boston, she was studying under some of the greatest thinkers in the country—and, in the case of James and Santayana, two of the most respected minds in the world—a much bigger step than that from the Adirondacks to New York. In truth, she had moved into another dimension of intellectuality, one that would soon place her among modern writers and artists who sought in their art to cut through to the essence of their subjects, rather than to register, camera-like, a "realistic" representation.

Jeanne's studies also gave more definition to her own philosophical and religious thoughts. She identified with James,[16] who returned nearly every summer to his camp in the Keene Valley region of the High Peaks in the Adirondacks "hungering

Jeanne riding side saddle in Back Bay, Boston, 1909. Photographer unknown.

for . . . the smell of the spruce, the feel of the moss, the sound of the cataract, the bath in the waters, the divine outlook from the cliff or hill top over the unbroken forest. . . ."[17] Jeanne herself returned each year to Crane Mountain in Johnsburg, where she had lived with relatives as a child; like James, she found something in the mountains that she could not find elsewhere.[18] For her, though, it was more than a retreat from the city, or the kind of search for picturesque beauty of lakes or pantheistic deity in the sublime landscape of the High Peaks that lured the romantics to the wilderness.[19] Rather, it was a return to the land where she had first learned to live with nature. She was at home in the harsh environment of the mountains; she understood the cyclical death-and-rebirth patterns that were apparent with the changing seasons, the growth and harvesting of crops, the habits of the predatory animals in the forests, and the replenishing of the soil from decaying trees and crumbling rock. It was there, in her beloved mountains, that she sensed the interrelationship and interdependency of all living things[20]—values that conservationists would articulate formally more than half a century later with the passage of the National Wilderness Act. It was there, too, she found her own strength and renewal.[21] The mountains provided the foundation for her belief that matter and spirit were not separate, but one substance: what was matter was also spirit, and vice versa.[22] This belief was perhaps best expressed in a poem of creation she wrote years later, and which was published posthumously in a collection of her spiritual poems entitled *Awakening Grace:*[23]

Where You Shall Find Him

Unless you perceive Him in all things
   you do not perceive Him.
His image is in the sky and on the earth
   and under the earth.
It is set on every star and on every point of
   light in the heavens:
In the small and the large and the infinite
   you will find Him.
He is not for times and occasions, nor
   for years, nor ages, nor eons.
He is the eternal, the everlasting, alike
   for the measurable and the unmeasured.

His signet is on every leaf, on each
   flower of the field;
On every blade of grass . . . in color,
   in light, in fragrance.
Find Him on the butterfly's wing, with the firefly
   that illumines the night;
In the faces of men and women and in
   the smiles of children,
In all that has been created and in all
   that awaits creation.
Unless you perceive Him in all things,
   You do not perceive Him.

Jeanne's studies in Boston impelled her into journalism—this time not as a model or layout assistant, but as a writer. Jeanne had always loved to write. By the time she was eight she was sending her parents long, informative letters about her schooling and about her activities while she was living with relatives. She read whatever she could find and tried her own hand at writing stories and poems and novels. She submitted articles to papers. (Her mother had made sure that Jeanne knew about the new "women's magazines" that were proliferating on the newsstands and about the increasing number of women who were holding editorial and writing jobs.[24]) Jeanne's first two years in the city probably overlapped those of the writer Willa Cather, who was there on assignment for *McClure's Magazine* to research and rewrite a story on the life of Mary Baker Eddy and the Christian Science Church that had been

A World War I correspondent, Jeanne pretended to be a tourist at Stonehenge while the Kitchener armies drilled on the Salisbury Plain opposite (1914). Photographer unknown. Courtesy of Paul Schaefer.

prepared by Georgine Milmine. In addition to her outstanding reputation as a journalist and critic, Cather was a distinguished creative writer. In Boston, Cather had become a close friend of the writer Sarah Orne Jewett,[25] and Jeanne's awareness of these two women would become apparent during the next two decades.

Jeanne became a reporter for the *Boston-American* and then moved to *The American Review of Reviews*. She returned to New York in 1911 to work with its editor, Dr. Albert Shaw, on the ten-volume set of the *Photographic History of the Civil War*, featuring Mathew Brady's magnificent photographs.[26] Jeanne was eventually to become the literary editor of Shaw's prestigious magazine, which focused on government, economics, and foreign affairs, carried articles on education, religion, and sports, and ran a major section entitled "New Books." The magazine had the largest circulation in the country among nonfiction periodicals, and Shaw was considered one of the finest editors in the business.

Jeanne's career with *The American Review of Reviews* lasted about eleven years. Journalism was challenging and exciting; it placed her on the forefront of contemporary thought and action. Moreover, it permitted her to combine her unique ability to recognize significant ideas and events with her impressive writing style. She worked closely with Shaw and certainly influenced the cultural direction of the magazine. In addition to eight to twelve pages of book reviews and poetry criticism every issue, she wrote about the avant-garde in art and literature, about woman's issues, about education, about the theater. She wrote under a number of different names: Jeanne Robert, Robert Foster, and Jeanne Robert Foster. In addition, she traveled to Europe three times for extended stays on magazine business: to survey public housing in the British Isles; to secure the Lincoln cartoons from the Bibliotheque Nationale in Paris; and as a World War I correspondent in England, sending stories and pictures back to Shaw. Ireland, England, Scotland, Wales, and France became her "beat."[27] Her duties led her to meet many outstanding figures of the day, and her charm and keen intellect soon turned such brief meetings into enduring friendships. Her work became important in another sense during this period, for she found that she could no longer depend upon her husband's support: he was now an elderly invalid with very limited resources who spent much of his time in hospitals and health spas.[28] Although of a demanding nature, Foster did permit Jeanne the freedom she needed to pursue her career and to earn enough not only to support herself but also to send needed money back to her family in Schenectady. Jeanne continued to be the financial as well as the emotional mainstay of the family, and she returned frequently to Schenectady and the Adirondacks. (Shaw could appreciate Jeanne's affinity for the mountains: his own summer home was on Schroon Lake, not far from Chestertown.[29])

Back in New York, Jeanne frequented Petitpas' restaurant, one of the intellectual conclaves of the period. Here, the literary and artistic leaders of the day hovered around the venerable John Butler Yeats, the well-known Irish portrait painter and father of the poet William Butler Yeats. John Sloan was a part of that group. He was one of the eight members of the so-called Ash Can School, which challenged the artistic standards of the National Academy of Design. "The Eight," as they were commonly called, drew upon the realism of the city for their subject matter, rather than upon the traditional landscapes and lyrical subjects then considered acceptable by the Academy. Their collaboration and independent exhibitions eventually led to the famous "Armory Show" of 1913, formally called the International Exhibition of Modern Art, which introduced America to the "isms" of modern artists and profoundly affected the direction of American art. Jeanne spent a great deal of time at this

John Butler Yeats

This unfinished drawing of Jeanne was on John Butler Yeats's drawing board at the time of his death in 1922.

controversial show, partly because of her expanding interest in art and partly because she had badgered Shaw into letting her do a story on the exhibition for the *Review of Reviews*.[30]

Jeanne became a close personal friend of the elder Yeats, who is remembered today for his writings and conversations as much as for his art. Besides joining him for dinners at the restaurant, she took him to meetings of the Poetry Society of America and other affairs of interest to him.[31] For his part, Yeats admired Jeanne's intelligence as much as her beauty. In a letter to his son dated May 10, 1914, Yeats commented on "A young lady . . . who writes (and writes well) all the poetical criticism in *Review of Reviews*. . . . [She] is a Mrs. Foster and [is] extraordinarily pretty and clever. . . . She comes from very poor people in the Adirondacks. . . . It is so rare to find so much really strong intellect with kindness and affection. . . . She has dignity and sense, and something remains to her from the spartan days when she had to work all day in her own poor home."[32] He could have added that Jeanne often posed for him. They developed a friendship that would last until his death in 1922, when she cared for him in his final illness and arranged for his burial next to the Foster family plot in the Chestertown Rural Cemetery in the town of her childhood. After Yeats died, Jeanne wrote a poem about him that was published in *The New York Times*. Ezra Pound was to write to John Quinn, one of Yeats's patrons and one of the Armory Show's strongest supporters, that the poem was "the best thing of her[s] I have seen."[33]

In 1916 Jeanne published *Wild Apples* and *Neighbors of Yesterday* (both published by Sherman, French and Company, Boston). The first was a collection of lyric poetry, and the second a series of true narrative verse stories about the settlers in the Adirondacks. Her work received positive reviews in papers and magazines across the country, and in a way it completed a trilogy of distinguished literary portraits by American women. Jewett had published *The Country of the Pointed Firs* in 1896; Cather had published *O Pioneers!* in 1913. The three women focused on the lives of the early settlers who had lived closely with nature—the sea off the coast of Maine, the prairie of Nebraska, and the mountains of northern New York, respectively. Yet each captured in her work universal human values and the self-reliant spirit of American pioneers. Their work, the culmination of an American feminine literary tradition that had begun in the 1830s,[34] was soon followed by a return to regionalism in literature and art by American male artists during the decades ahead as the country abandoned its pre-war idealism and grimly questioned the human price the country had paid for its share of victory in World War I. (It is interesting to note that Jeanne was thirty-seven when her first books came out.)

Through Yeats, Jeanne met John Quinn, the New York lawyer, art patron, and one of the major backers of the Armory Show. She had not met Quinn when she wrote an article about the show entitled "Art Revolutionists on Exhibition" for the April 1913, issue of the *Review of Reviews*. Yeats became very ill in 1918, and Quinn phoned Jeanne asking her to oversee his care.[35] With common interests in the Irish literary revival and in art generally, Jeanne and Quinn quickly developed a close relationship that would last until Quinn's death in 1924, and whose spiritual essence would stay with Jeanne until her own death nearly fifty years later. She found in Quinn a man of vision, a man who loved art and beauty and who was able to recognize genius.[36] With Quinn, as with Yeats and with some of the other great men she knew, Jeanne found in their creativity a unity of spirit and matter that she sought throughout her long life. She dealt with such a man on this level, with the result that theirs was not a personal relationship in the usual sense, nor in any way a competition for recognition or position. (For Jeanne's part, at least, she was satisfied with the recognition she received from her writing and editorial work. She was listed in the 1922–23 edition of *Who's Who in America*, and was generally recognized as one of the country's leading woman poets.[37])

Between 1918 and 1924, Jeanne worked closely with Quinn as he assembled what was to be the most significant collection of contemporary French art in America at that time. She traveled in Europe with him three times, talking with artists and working with Henri-Pierre Roché in the selection of work.[38] Her intelligence, beauty, and charm counterbalanced Quinn's somewhat abrasive manner, and she was able to cultivate friendships with Pablo Picasso, Constantin Brancusi, André Derain, Gwen

During a trip to France with John Quinn in 1923 Jeanne (second from right) played golf at St. Cloud with sculptor Constantin Brancusi (fourth from left), art agent Henri-Pierre Roché (fifth from left), and the composer Erik Satie (sixth from left). Photographer unknown.

John, and other prominent artists. She also associated with some of the major literary figures of the day, including William Butler Yeats, James Joyce, T. S. Eliot, Ezra Pound, and Ford Madox Ford, some of whom she had met in the course of previous trips abroad.[39] Jeanne was readily accepted into their circles, since she was extremely cultured and well-read, aware of what was happening around the world, and adapted naturally to a European setting that held attitudes about women that differed from those at home. She posed for Derain and John, had long conversations with Ford and Pound. Later, after she had returned to New York, she maintained an active correspondence with many of them.

With a reorganization at the *Review of Reviews* in 1922 Jeanne resigned from her position with the magazine. She became the American editor of the short-lived *transatlantic review*, the legendary "little magazine" edited in Paris by Ford Madox Ford. Today, Ford is credited with being one of the key figures in the renaissance of post-World War I English literature, and in particular for his sponsorship of American writers who had fled—primarily to Paris—at the end of the war.[40] Jeanne continued her association with Pound and served as his agent in the United States for a time.[41] At the same time, she continued with her own free-lance writing, including an article about Brancusi's sculpture for the May 1922 issue of *Vanity Fair* magazine. In 1923 Boni and Liveright published her third volume of poetry, *Rock Flower,* and Horace Liveright, one of the many New York publishers anxious to publish the work of modern writers,[42] asked her to work for him. However, she refused.[43] For one thing, Quinn's health—always problematic since his operation for cancer in 1918—was failing. Desperately, she fought to keep him alive, and managed to take him to Crane Mountain in the Adirondacks—a place where she had so often found physical and spiritual strength.[44] Quinn had often vacationed in the Adirondacks with his sister's family, but he had never before had to look for the life-giving forces that Jeanne felt

John Quinn standing at the edge of the pond near the summit of Crane Mountain in the Adirondacks, where Jeanne had taken him in 1923. Photographer unknown. Courtesy of Warder Cadbury.

were inherent in the mountains. On his deathbed, Quinn asked Jeanne to edit the vast correspondence dealing with his art and manuscript collections. For a year, she worked to put his papers in order, after which they were accepted by the New York Public Library and sealed for fifty years.[45] With Quinn's death and the liquidation of his estate, a part of Jeanne died. She had walked side by side with one of the world's visionaries in the areas of art and literature, and she knew that America was not yet ready to accept his modern art collection. An auction would bring but a fraction of the collection's value and would obscure the memory of the man who assembled it.[46] Jeanne had reason to doubt that she would live to see Quinn receive the recognition he deserved.

With Yeats and Quinn dead, and with most of the rest of her artistic and literary associates an ocean away, Jeanne's life became more routine. The country had changed after the war: the national mood had sobered, and a degree of disillusionment had set it. Paris had replaced New York as the cultural magnet for America, where many of the young writers were in rebellion against Prohibition and swept up in the backlash of violence that hit the country after the success of the Russian Revolution. Jeanne was in her mid-forties by this time, and family responsibilities were demanding more and more of her time and energy. She concentrated on her free-lance work and her own writing. She was listed in *Who's Who Among North American Authors* in 1925, the year she wrote *Marthe*—a one-act play that won national recognition two years later when it was published under the pen name of Noel Armstrong in *Fifty More Contemporary One-Act Plays* by D. Appleton-Century Company, New York, 1927. From 1927 to 1932, Jeanne traveled between New York and Schenectady, caring for some members of her family who suffered from tuberculosis. Her mother—an active suffragist who had been a Socialist Party candidate for state senator—died in 1927, and in the next few years her brother, father, and husband were also to die. With the financial crash of 1929 and the resulting Depression, Jeanne closed up her New York apartment and moved north, in 1932.[47] When she left New York she quietly closed her door to one of the most exciting eras in contemporary art and literature in the United States and abroad. She took with her to Schenectady her memories, her cherished letters, and pieces of artwork that reflected her participation in a young country half-intoxicated on the heady wine of its talented youth.

For many people acquainted with Jeanne Robert Foster, her return to Schenectady meant the fading into an obscure position with the Schenectady Municipal Housing Authority, where she served as a tenant-relations counselor from 1938 until her retirement in 1955. For those familiar with her sensitive and compassionate *Neighbors of Yesterday*, however, this was not a surprising move, but rather the surfacing of yet another dimension of her personality—yet another manifestation of the spirited child who had traveled through the Adirondacks at the side of her lumberjack father.[48] The Depression had taken its toll on America, with millions jobless, homeless, and hungry. Jeanne could not forget her subsistence life in the mountains, where the houses were usually inferior to the barns. Nor could she forget the neat cottages provided for the laborers of the Lever plant in Liverpool, the cleared slum districts and new plans for public housing in London, Manchester, and Birmingham, and the corps of visiting nurses in Glasgow who checked the eyes and diet of the children living in group housing. What had really moved her was the vision of George Russell ("A.E."), who headed the co-operative housing movement in Ireland. In his company she had seen the simple thatched cottages, often with muddy yards and dirt floors and lacking even the basic sanitary amenities, leaving the children unprotected from the ravages of disease.[49] Jeanne felt that the American government should provide decent housing for those set back by the times, at least until they could get on their feet again. With the knowledge she had gained from her survey of public housing in the British Isles, her work in New York City with the Sing Sing Social Service Bureau, and her experience as a "Lady on the Block" (the precursor of the social worker), she passed the qualifying exams for appointment to the Schenectady Municipal Housing Authority,[50] the first housing authority set up in New York State under the federal public-housing program of the New Deal.[51] This piece of New Deal legislation marked a major shift in the involvement of the federal government in planning economic and social welfare reform on a national level. Jeanne was fifty-nine years of age when she began this third career.

Jeanne was especially concerned with the problems of the elderly, many of whom were alone and with little income. She felt that their housing should be adapted to accommodate their diminishing physical energy, and that they should be encouraged to participate in the social, educational, and recreational activities of the community.[52] During her seventeen years with the MHA Jeanne pushed for the first low-income housing designed for the elderly in the state and organized the first Golden Age Club in 1947. The club—begun in the community room of one of the housing projects—eventually grew into the Schenectady Senior Citizens' Center, with its own facilities, professional staff, and programs.[53] With her quiet dignity, Jeanne was an inspiration to those she worked with—few if any of whom knew of her exciting years in New York City and abroad.[54] In a letter to Joseph Mosarra, written on April 17, 1967, she revealed in her praise for him her own deep-rooted motivation

Jeanne's forward-thinking work coupled with her concern for the elderly earned her Schenectady's Senior Citizen of the Year Award in 1959. She was eighty years of age when Mayor Sheldon (*right*) presented the award. Mrs. Wesley J. Meng, president of the Schenectady Society of Senior Citizens, looks on. Two years later Jeanne received the Schenectady Patroon Award, the city's highest honor. Photograph courtesy of *The Schenectady Gazette*.

for this work: "The members [of the Center] are so fortunate in having you for Executive Director . . . you who realized how important the rescue of the elderly—or indeed anyone—is from their *self imprisonment* and their energies turned into proper channels. I thought of where the aged were when I was a small girl in an Adirondack community and compared their sorry lives with the lives of the elderly today . . . and thanked God for the inspiring orientation of service and love that you so freely give." Her own leadership was recognized when she received Schenectady's Senior Citizen of the Year Award in 1959, followed by the Schenectady Patroon Award—the city's highest honor—in 1961.

In the mid-fifties a few acquaintances in Schenectady began to learn about her New York experiences when Jeanne mentioned that Aline Saarinen had contacted her. Saarinen had begun the preparation of her book *The Proud Possessors*, which included a chapter on John Quinn. With the Quinn papers still sealed in the New York Public

Library, she depended on Jeanne to a great extent for information on Quinn. Jeanne was pleased that, at long last, Quinn was being recognized for the critical role he had played in the development of modern art and literature. Thus, the door that she had quietly shut when she left New York was again ajar: sufficient time had passed that scholars and historians were trying to piece together the story of the avant-garde, and people were coming to her for her remembrances of Yeats, Ford, Quinn, Gwen John—and about John's famous brother, Augustus John. References to Jeanne began to appear in books and articles dealing with artists and writers she had known during the period she lived in New York.[55] And she too was beginning to receive some recognition of her work behind the scenes during this pioneering period of art and literature: Union College would award her an honorary doctorate degree in 1970.

Jeanne's writing had become more of an avocation once she accepted full-time responsibilities with the Schenectady Municipal Housing Authority. She continued to write, however, and submitted her work to various magazines for publication. It was her hope that after her retirement in 1955 she could spend more time on her poetry. She won first prize commendations in 1957 from both the Pennsylvania Poetry Society and the Tennessee Poetry Society, and was listed in the International *Who's Who in Poetry* (London) in 1958. She taught poetry courses at the Senior Citizens Center; edited several volumes of her students' work; gave lectures in poetry

At ninety-one years of age Jeanne was granted an honorary doctorate from Union College, recognizing her contributions to one of the most exciting and innovative periods in art and literature. Dr. Harold Martin, president of the college, stands behind Jeanne's right shoulder. Photographer unknown.

and philosophy at the local poetry society; and helped many area poets, college students, and professors with their literary efforts.

In 1963 Jeanne's reputation was renewed by the republication of *Neighbors of Yesterday* by Riedinger and Riedinger Limited of Schenectady. My parents, Tex and Ruth Riedinger, saw her book about the Adirondacks as an important piece of regional literature, especially in view of the attention being focused on New York State's stringent "Forever Wild" constitutional covenant. This—the oldest and most significant single piece of land preservation legislation in the nation—served as the model for the pending National Wilderness Act (that would pass in 1964). Articles and stories about Jeanne and her Adirondack poetry began to appear in newspapers and magazines, and the reviews were as favorable as they had been after the first publication in 1916. At last she was recognized as the voice of her mountains, just as Cather was identified with Nebraska and Jewett with Maine; no longer was she sequestered behind the doors of her Schenectady home. Buoyed by this new-found recognition, Jeanne concentrated her efforts on finishing her second volume of Adirondack poetry, begun years before and worked on sporadically ever since. In a letter to Ruth Riedinger (February 15, 1961), she commented on her progress:

> To go back to the Adirondack book, words come easily but when, one is older and interruptions are frequent, to evoke the image often takes time. For instance: I have written the story of "The Dancing Man" of Chestertown five times. Not until I was under "his skin" could I have the poem. Of course, I had to write of him from legend; I did not know him. If I had, the task would not have been difficult.

Behind Jeanne's desire to complete this book were a sincere appreciation of and devotion to the Adirondacks, and to wilderness generally. For her it meant the completion of a life cycle that began at the base of Crane Mountain, and would only end in the Foster family plot in Chestertown. In her lifetime she had traveled across the United States and Canada, and to Europe. She had been in contact with some of the most progressive minds in Boston, New York, London, and Paris. She had seen the gentler traditions of an agrarian society give way to the aggressiveness of technological society that placed men on the moon. She had seen many wilderness regions across the nation yield to the bulldozer and chain saw as America exploited its natural resources. And she had carefully watched the connotation of "wilderness" change as New York State placed more and more of its critical watershed mountain areas under constitutional protection. It was from this perspective that she commented on the life of the early Adirondack settlers of her childhood, men and women who lived at the edge of the vast northern wilderness of New York before the turn of the twentieth century. To her long-time acquaintance Sara Bowyer O'Connor she wrote on October 6, 1962:

> I am passionately devoted to the Adirondacks; they are in my blood. I have seen many groups of mountains in various parts of the world but none so beautiful. I am revising a new book of true Adirondack stories (in verse). It is not probable that I shall be watching the seasons very long, but I hope God will let me finish this book.

As time and health began to give way, Jeanne reached again to the mountains—this time through Paul Schaefer, New York State conservationist—for the strength to complete her book. She corresponded frequently with him, applauding his efforts to keep intact the "Forever Wild" clause that kept the New York State Forest Preserve from being lumbered and many of the wild rivers from being dammed. In the 1920s Jeanne had worked closely with John G. Agar in New York.[56] Agar was president of the Association for the Protection of the Adirondacks, a powerful group that acted as legislative watchdog for the New York State Forest Preserve, when the first major threat of dams in the Adirondacks occurred. It was during this period that the modern wilderness aesthetic began to emerge, positing that wilderness areas should be left undisturbed, wherein man could observe the perfection, harmony, and interdependence of all of nature.[57] Since man was a part of nature, his dominion included the responsibility for its preservation. As early as the 1930s, Schaefer had fought to define "wilderness" in the public's mind, and in the 1940s and 1950s he was the driving force in the eleven-year battle that eventually succeeded in banning the construction of dams in the New York State Forest Preserve. In the 1950s, finally, his appointment to the special advisory committee to the New York State Joint Legislative Committee on Natural Resources gave the modern wilderness aesthetic an unwavering voice on a public body.[58] Jeanne knew that Schaefer understood her love for the mountains and the wilderness. In a letter to him on September 22, 1969, she stated:

> My second book of true Adirondack stories lies here unrevised. Your letters have given me courage to go on with it. The ballads are easy; the difficult part is the reproduction of the actual speech of those I knew.

For both, Crane Mountain held a special meaning and created a common bond. On October 11, 1969, she wrote to him, "Because you are so much one with this strange soul of the mountain, whatever I can do in the short time I have, I shall do for you. I will start work on my text and difficult meter." She explained this in more detail to him on October 28, 1969:

> When I sent you my first tribute, I should have known your thought was encased in Teilhard de Chardin's consciousness. I did know in a way, writing on the "magnificence of your mind." Of all the brilliant minds I have been permitted to know, only two shared what I now call "our consciousness," the poet and mystic William Butler Yeats and the practical builder of the Irish Co-Operative Movement, who built clean beautiful cottages for the peasants in Ireland, A. E., George Russell, poet and painter. Although I could not get books by de Chardin until recently, I knew some of his beliefs. You belong to his new order, those who communicate with and know planetary consciousness and find—as I found in the wilderness and my mountain—a communication far more uplifting and eternal than the creeds of men. That I now may share this consciousness with you gives me my happiness. I hope this knowledge can be reflected in my new manuscript. Unless it is, I would prefer to destroy it.

Unfortunately, Jeanne did not live to complete her book. She died in 1970 at the age of ninety-one, in ill health and concerned to the end about the disposition of the balance of her priceless collection of letters and artwork from her New York period. She had managed to place the Pound material with Houghton Library at Harvard University, but she wavered about the rest. She left the balance of her material to a number of individuals, hoping they would make it available to others.

My mother was one of the beneficiaries: she received a part of Jeanne's own literary legacy, which contained many unpublished poems and prose pieces, including the narrative verses that Jeanne had set aside for her second Adirondack book, as well as countless letters, scrapbooks, photographs, artwork, and other personal items.

My mother died in 1983 after a long illness. (My father had died in 1968, a few years after the release of *Neighbors of Yesterday*.) I moved the boxes and boxes of material labeled "Jeanne Robert Foster" from the attic and spread their contents out on the study floor. Hour after hour I read about this woman whom I had visited on Sunday evenings, sat next to at Thanksgiving and Christmas Eve dinners, corre-sponded with in college, and drove to poetry meetings. The image of Jeanne which emerged from the yellowed newspaper clippings and old photographs was not what I remembered of the quiet, gentle woman who sent me material on Joyce and Pound to include in my college research papers, critiqued my writing, and encouraged me to continue my sculpture and riding. Here before me was a Jeanne Robert Foster I did not know. Here in scattered array were her unpublished Adirondack poems and bits and pieces of a story that told why in the final years she struggled to finish her book. At long last I began to understand the meaning of her letter (September 6, 1962) to me:

> This Pound paper is so well done. Begin the pattern again . . . go to Paris, meet your contemporaries—the writers, the artists and build *your house of memories* for the future. No matter what happens, I am still walking on the Champs Elysee with Pound, listening to Joyce in his apartment, at dinner with Ford Madox Ford and the current wife, late breakfast at the Cafe Dome, living, breathing life as it exists in Paris. You will have *your heroes* to remember, *your days and nights of adventure,* your thrills to ART, your own bouquets. Don't settle with life for its small change; reach for the gold.

There had always been something in her letter that spoke to me. But now I had to know more about the intense child—there in the picture before me—who stood with her parents and sister in front of the log house in the Adirondacks: What had moti-vated her to reach for her gold?

Adirondack Portraits: A Piece of Time is that story, her story. It is a selection from Jeanne's unpublished poems, supplemented by photographs that she helped to take as a small child, by prose selections about her Adirondack life, and by excerpts from her extensive correspondence. The work is arranged chronologically, following Jeanne through Essex, Warren, and Hamilton counties, New York. Her writing captures both the pioneer spirit of her youth and her love for and understanding of the mountain region. The photographs add a startling note of realism of time and place, while the excerpts from her letters reveal some of the influences that helped her move from a rough physical existence in the mountains to a place in the foreground of literature, art, and social reform—and that helped her attain a measure of independence and professional recognition truly exceptional for a woman of her generation. It is the combination of these disparate elements that gives, finally, an insight into Jeanne's spirituality.

Most of the photographs were taken by the Reverend Osmond David Putnam (1861–1926), Jeanne's second cousin, between 1885 and 1887. He earned money for his theological education by taking pictures with a 5 × 8 inch camera and gelatin glass-plate negatives. Blessed with a critical eye for composition and good technical skills, he produced many good pictures. His Adirondack photographs are probably all that remain of his work. His granddaughter, Myrtle Putnam Buyce, believes that his other work and equipment were lost in a fire that destroyed the family's farmhouse in Wilton, New York, in the 1920s. Fortunately, he had given more than a hundred of his Adirondack negatives to his brother Elliot, who in turn gave them to Jeanne. (Her identification appears directly below the photographs.)

Sixteen years have passed since Jeanne's death. In that time, the pages of history and literature have been writ large with the contributions of women. Many outstanding women—who for years stood in the shadows of men—are now getting long-overdue recognition. One of these—Jeanne Robert Foster—will be remembered, not for her singular contribution as writer, model, editor, and social worker, but rather as a remarkable person whose long and varied life was a microcosm of a country coming of age.

I can confidently leave the last word on Jeanne to Paul Schaefer, the eminent New York State conservationist, who was her close friend:

> Born in the shadow of what would become her most beloved mountain, Jeanne Robert Foster grew up in an impoverished family that had to "farm her out" to ease its financial burdens. Shining through her hardscrabble life, however, came the roar of majestic rivers, the sight of rainbows on high mountain cataracts and of deer bounding off through the dense woods, and the bewitching fragrance of a wilderness close at hand. The lovely infinities of Nature she saw against the backdrop of an early life devoid of a normal family security.
>
> Her appreciation of the simple men and women who made that early life not merely bearable but exciting provided her with a basis for friendship with some of the world's most famous and most gifted individuals. Her early experiences with people and Nature in the Adirondacks provided a rich background for the intellectual accomplishments of her later, very rewarding years. The substance of this richness will be found in and between the lines of this journal.

Noel Riedinger-Johnson

Adirondack Portraits

A Piece of Time[59]

"Did you see him, Francis?" "Yes, I found him.
He wasn't sick—at least nothing special;
He's always been weakly, living alone
Up there in the old house his father left,
Getting his own meals, poor ones most likely—
And full of queer ideas."

       "Well, his father
Was a queer one too in this neighborhood;
Didn't half-run his farm, and sold his wool
To buy a telescope and sat up nights
Peering at the stars and thinking they had
Something to do with life down here."
"I know, and his father wrote a book once,
Something wild about the stars and the earth
And got it printed, wasting all he had."

"What did he have to say?" "Just crazy talk.
There isn't a rod of land in his name
Except the acre the old house stands on,
And that is mortgaged to the hilt, I know,
But to hear him talk, he *owns* the township
And the county and the state—everything.
He's crazy as a loon and he won't change.
So long as he is mild and lives up there
And takes it out in talk, let him go on."

"What does he say he owns?" "Well, the first thing
He calls a '*piece of time*'; he means the years
Since he was born; and then he raves along
And even names your flowers out by the fence
As his, and Mill Creek Pond . . . a silver maple there.
The Johnsburg Woods. Mary, he even says
He owns the Hudson. And every last white pine
On our Crane Mountain. Says they came to him
With his own '*piece of time*.' He talks about dreams.
He talks of leaving what he never had
To his good friends. Mary, the man is daft."

"Well, I can see how he takes comfort there
Thinking he owns the world. I'll pick some pinks
For him. He's harmless. When you go next time
To see whether he's sick or well,
I'll send him some preserves and berry pie."

3

A beautiful view from the ridge opposite Crane Mountain. The country between the ridge and Mill Creek Pond (Garnet Lake Road) is bisected by Kenyontown Road, Town of Johnsburg, Warren County, New York.

The Adirondack Mountains were long considered to be one of America's last frontiers.* *As late as 1830, the vast, nine-thousand-square-mile wilderness in northern New York had still not been mapped, nor were there records of its having been traversed. Most of the early settlers bypassed this rugged, almost impenetrable mountain region and moved westward to more fertile lowlands via the Mohawk River, the Erie Canal, and the St. Lawrence River. A few hardy lumbermen and farmers, however, followed the Adirondack waterways into the mountains and settled in the valleys. As time went on, these early settlements remained isolated from the tourists who flocked to the shores of the mountain lakes and swift rivers, or tried to climb the lofty peaks. Lumbering and farming remained the economic underpinnings of such communities. While the lumber industry was controlled by a few men who used it to become wealthy, most of the work was done by settlers who labored as lumberjacks, skidders, and log drivers during the winter months and returned to their farms in spring and summer to work their fields.*

In 1813 certain rivers were designated public highways that lumbermen could use to move the lighter coniferous logs out of the mountains. Thirty percent of the existing forest consisted of conifers that could be cut and then floated downstream to market. By 1885, an estimated two-thirds of the softwood forests in the Adirondacks had been lumbered—and the grim effects were being signaled by the ravaging forest fires in the mountains and the diminishing water supply in the rivers and canals.[60]

*Text printed in roman type in the main section of this book (i.e., following the introduction and up to the play *Marthe*) was written by Jeanne Robert Foster. Text in italic type in this section was prepared by Noel Riedinger-Johnson.

Letter to Ruth Riedinger

What is this I hear from North Creek,
Bakers Mills? Did you not know
I own that territory beyond a doubt?
When I was born in Johnsburg who could know
Camps would spring up, dude ranches, game preserves?

Sodom and Bakers Mills were wild those days.
It took a man with strong and steady nerves
To argue with a man from Sodom town.
As time went on I took three counties over,
Essex and Warren and wild Hamilton,
And sealed them in a book. Now you're a rover
And set up camp where the old shanties stood
And where men "peeled bark" for the tanneries.

I can tell you some tales—tall tales; I've written them
For my new book; there are so many ties
With soil and mountain roads and country stores
And with folks who lie sleeping that my heart
Thrills even to the names: Crane Mountain, Gore,
And "No. 11"; they became a part
Of all I was and all I hoped to be:
The woolen factory once at Johnsburg
Where later on they made fine calico.
The lead mine on the mountain, the paint bed,
The garnet outcrops, hemlocks—row on row.

Some day I hope to take you on a tour
Of my three-county farm, and show you where
The southern slaves slept overnight in peace
Before—beneath wild hay, a hidden fare—
My great grandsire brought them on to North Creek.
The "Underground" at Johnsburg never failed.
The old church that great grandsire built still lifts
Its Georgian steeple; there no farmer quailed
Before assault, and on Emancipation Day they
Set candles in the windows to proclaim
That man's triumphant spirit rules his clay.

I grant you tenancy. My ownership
Is now known only to the blowing wind:
Old shanty days, old settlers, old log barns,
And houses, they have vanished out of mind.
But I have told those who will carry me
When my eyes close to fold me tenderly
In some wild mountain valley where the wind
Will sing—through pines—a requiem over me.

As time went on I took three counties over,
Essex . . .

In 1881, after years in lumber camps, Jeanne's father decided to farm. He moved his family to the Town of Minerva, Essex County, in the east-central Adirondacks, a triangular region roughly outlined by the paths of the Hudson and Schroon rivers north of their confluence. Nearby, his grandfather, Aaron Oliver, had once held title to more than one thousand acres of land that he had secured when he migrated from Vermont after the American Revolution. One of the photographs shows the Oliver family in front of the Burto log house where they lived until Jeanne was almost eight.

The Olmstedville section of the 1876 Essex County map shows the Burto house and the locations of the other settlers, mostly Irish, who lived close to Trout Brook—the Coles, Suprenants, Wamsleys, and Wilsons. In her peoms Jeanne creates portraits of many of these people, often interchanging names to obscure real identities, but always retaining the values they gained from their close relationship with the land.

Olmstedville, Town of Minerva, Essex County, New York

Many of the early settlers who had worked on farms elsewhere came to Minerva because they could buy land cheap. They came mainly from Vermont, Canada, and Ireland, and they were willing to work the thin, rocky Adirondack soil because they could own the land.[61]

Like many other small villages in the mountains, Olmstedville was built near a stream that could supply the power needed for the mills. William Hill was given 200 acres of land in 1804 to build a grist mill on Minerva Creek to grind buckwheat and corn into flour and cornmeal for the settlers. Later, he built a sawmill to provide the lumber for their homesteads.[62] Photograph courtesy of Andrew Holloran

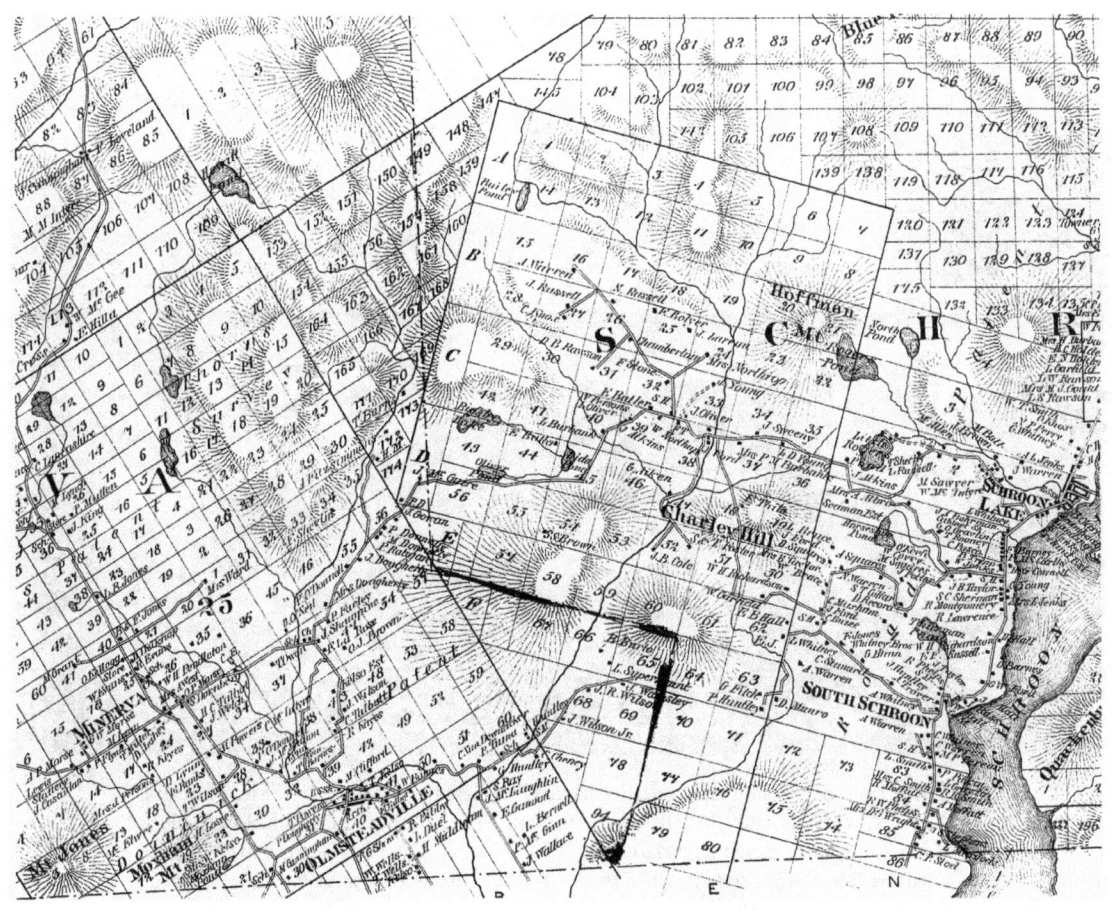

Detail from *New Topographical Atlas of Essex County, New York, 1876*, printed by
O. W. Gray and Son, Philadelphia, Pa.

O. D. Putnam

The Louis Suprenant House, Leonardsville, Town of Minerva, Essex County, New York. Now only brush covers the site. Left: father, Louis, holding black Canadian horse. Stoop left: daughter, Etta; cousin, Anna McGinn; son, Modeste with violin. Stoop right: wife, Emily Suprenant; Mrs. Anna LaRose; Minnie McGinn with son, William.

The families of the early settlers usually remained very close, with grown children and their families often settling near their parents. When the father died, the family holdings were generally divided among the children, and the mother joined the household of one of her offspring. The families shared the heavy work, and stood by one another in times of joy and sorrow. Music played an important part in the lives of many families, providing entertainment and relaxation after the long days of hard work.

Neighbors

The word "neighbors" don't mean much to most folks,
Not unless you lived back in the North Woods.
And the way things are going there won't be woods
Very long, or wilderness; it'll be
Imitation ranches, and ski runs, and places
Called by names that the folks who lived there
Years and years ago never heard of.
But lovely things vanish; flowers that grew everywhere
Hide for a little while, and where once were meadows
With beaver dams, and streams crossing the roads
That the horses waded through with wagons,
They are going as the feet of destruction
And progress climb the high peaks.

There my neighborhood was—along Trout Brook.
You climbed the long hill to the Wilson farms.
Rob Wilson's was first; his wife Gussie Wilson,
She made rag rugs and carpeting; the parlor,
Closed nearly always, had a smell of herbs.
Next on the hill was Rob's brother Joe Wilson,
Not like Rob, stoutish but kind; his wife
Read an offer of a parlor suite for five dollars,
Sent away the hard-earned cash; they sent her
A doll's walnut suite covered with blue velvet.

Farther on, climbing the hill, was Charley Wilson.
His farm looked down upon the other farms
Of the valley; he had the neighborhood's respect.
His oldest son, Charley, in his Prince Albert
Looked after all the schools of the county.
His orchard was fenced with good board fencing.
He raised blue plums and sent us a pailful
At harvest time.

                    The road divided here.
On the high fork Old Man Wamsley lived
With his wife and daughters and son Wullie.
The Wilsons and the Wamsleys were Irish
From the north of Ireland. I heard them sing
The "Famine Song" their fathers had brought here.

> Oh, the praties they grow small
> Over here, over here.
> Oh, the praties they grow small
> Over here.
> Oh, the praties they grow small
> And they're failing in the fall
> And we eat them skins and all
> Over here.

I learned to sing it in the neighborhood.

The other fork of the road led down
To the Pat McGinn place, as it was called.
Before that it had been the Frank Oliver place.
And long ago it was called after the man
Who timbered and cut the stout logs and chinked
The crevices, Ben Burteau. This log house
Was the second one he built. The other
Was too far from the road, by the woods;
Now there is only a cellar hole left; roses
Bloom in the rich soil, wild red roses;
And an old spice apple tree hangs its branches
Over tall catnip and caraway still there.

Across the brook on a slope Louis Suprenant lived;
"France-French" he always said. His house was logs,
But he had covered the logs with siding
To be more genteel; he was a good neighbor.
Father and the sons, Modeste and Alfred,
Walked out each spring to river-driving
Carrying their own pike poles Louis had made.
Emily his wife was bent and crippled,
But his daughter Etta was beautiful,
Beautiful and kind. She loved small children,
Showed them how to find violets and woods-flowers,
And sang "Down in the Little Green Valley,"
One of the lost songs of a lovelorn maiden.
Louis had black Canadian horses
With divided manes; he sent up north for them.
They were better for farm work, Louis said.

Down the road farther, but still a neighbor,
Frank Gregory lived fronting beaver meadows
With his five children. Luddy and Sarah
Helped me to salt the sheep, and the twins
Came up and slept in my trundle bed whenever
The neighbors made a bee or helped haying.
There were no quarrels in the old neighborhood.
We shared what we had: apples, plums, and pears.
We gave honey, for my father kept bees;
Changed settings of eggs, quilted together.
The men raised barns and drank switchell
In the hayfield together; we were neighbors.

There are a few scattered oldsters left
Who remember the neighborhood
Where men and women walked on in kindness
Undisturbed, and later slept with their fathers
In quiet graveyards of the Wilderness.

14

Jen Murdock's Roosters

Nature don't listen to us very much.
When we tell her what to do, she veers off
On some road she had in her mind
Before we were born. Smart men tell us now
That they're digging down into her secrets,
But when they've dug out just how she does things
And set it all down, she'll pull out a trick
That's brand new.

        When I think about it all—
I remember Jen Murdock's hens; their eggs
Seemed to hatch mostly roosters, not pullets.
They were just barnyard fowls; you couldn't tell
What breed they were; they had mixed-up feathers,
But when one of them "set" and Jen gave her nest eggs
Expecting to raise some laying pullets,
Like as not she'd get a brood of roosters.

One day last spring Jen came down to my place
And said, "I want to borrow a setting of eggs;
There's something queer about my hens.
When their eggs hatch, the chicks are all roosters.
I've heard that round eggs will hatch out pullets.
So pick out thirteen round eggs—no long ones."
I brought out the egg crock and Jen picked up
A setting of *round* eggs.

        She was lucky:
They all hatched; she had thirteen fine chickens.
Her husband, Rob, built a new coop for them.
They grew fast, and when they were feathered out
Rob would listen at the coop now and then
And call: "Jen, you've got another rooster."
It went on until—there was no mistake—
Jen had twelve roosters out of round eggs.
One chick looked like a pullet; the next week
When Rob came into the house after milking,
"Guess what, Jen," he said. "*Your pullet's crowing*."

The Frank Oliver House, Leonardsville, Town of Minerva, Essex County, New York. Right: father, Frank Oliver, holds Nancy, the Hambletonian mare. Left: wife, Lucia [Lizzy Putnam] Oliver; child scratching head, Clara; and Julia Elizabeth Oliver [Jeanne Robert Foster] in calico dress and gingham apron.

This was the second house that Ben Burto built. The first was about one-eighth of a mile down the hill in back of our house in the pasture. The Burto name was then spelled the French way—Burteau. My father's aunt, Joanna Lavery, turned Ben off the place because he did not pay the interest on the mortgage. When he left he stood outside the house and cursed the place with black curses. I felt, because of his curses, we should never be happy there.[63]

16

The Old Log House

Long after it was built, the old house,
Made of stout logs chinked in with plaster,
Stood in the valley in the meadow land.
It had four rooms and a sweet-smelling loft
Reached by a ladder from the southern side.
There was no cellar, but a plank trapdoor
Out of the kitchen lifted on a hole where,
From the warmth of the good kitchen fire
That burned above, one could keep potatoes
Frost-free for the winter's use.
When I lived there the fireplace had been closed.
A reddened kitchen stove gave out the heat
And kept the kettles steaming that we filled
From the deep well a little from the door.
Dragging the heavy sweep to lift the pails
We brought the water through the single door.
When it was winter we hung comforters
Against the logs to keep out draughts and chill.

Summer was always cool in the log house.
The window in the kitchen faced the east.
We saw the sun rise over wooded hills.
The other windows, in rooms where we slept,
Looked out on the long mountain to the west
And the wood lot where the logs had been cut
To build the house; the cedars near the swamp
Had given cedar shingles for the roof,
Shaved by the neighbors who had made a bee
To help Ben Burteau build his fine log home.

There was a pen for pigs built out of logs,
And a frame barn my father raised with help
Of these same neighbors, and a corncrib on stilts
With the old handmade five-quart pans turned down
Above supporting timbers so the mice could not destroy
The food for cattle and for all the hens.

Around the house a low dirt banking ran
To keep out cold in winter. When the spring
Was late and work was heavy, it remained
Throughout the summer, and my mother flung
Petunia seed and pansies in the soil
So they cascaded through the summertime.
Beyond the wall and to the south and west
The purple lilacs grew and a young pear tree bloomed.

A sunken flowerbed held portulacas.
The only picture on the walls inside
Was my mother's marriage lines set in a frame
That held tintypes of the young lovers, made
Upon the day that they had pledged their love.
But on a shelf above the handmade couch there stood
A red glass vase my mother filled with blooms
And in the winter with the dried straw flowers.

Before the day began we looked due north,
Where Whiteface and old Marcy framed the north,
To see what weather promised for the day.
My father followed what old Whiteface told us then
Of storms or winds or snow or pleasant weather.

And winter evenings we sat round the stove
With apples from the cellar hold, beechnuts
From the woods, and at the end of day
After the sheep and cattle were all fed
My father read from our old Bible kept
Upon the shelf beside the vase of flowers.

The Apple-Eater

Cy Pritchard had heard about Johnny Appleseed
And how he went through the country leaving
A trail of apple trees. Cy followed his ways.
He had a big stomach for apple-eating.
He'd come to see you in the wintertime,
And when you brought up a pan of apples
(They kept perfect in those country cellars)
Cy would take out his pocket knife and pare
And eat a five-quart pan of apples.
He liked to go where folks had different kinds;
He liked Seek-No-Furthers and Gill Flowers and Greenings,
Tolman Sweets and Russets, pippins and spice apples.
If you had a Sheep's Nose, he'd pick that one
First of all, for he wanted to get seeds.
He'd put the seeds into a little bag and thank you.
He put them in good places up north,
Here, there, and everywhere, on the roadside,
Beside old houses folks had left for good
And along rail fences where they could grow.

He lived long enough to see some of them
Come into bearing. Most were wild apples,
Hard and sour, not fit for eating.
But here and there among his plantings
Was a good apple; that red sweet apple
Back of the schoolhouse was one Cy planted.
Its scions are scattered all over the North Woods.
I don't know how many people grafted from it.

I miss going down cellar in winter
To fetch Cy a pan of winter apples.
Perhaps his planting didn't do much good,
But he was lucky to have one sweet apple
Out of all his seeds. Some folks don't have that much
Left from all their planting in this world.

Jackson Balls

Francey Oliver ran the farm while his father lumbered
To support the five children he fathered
And his wife who had come from "down below"
And never worked like other farm women.
Francey was the oldest. When he was twelve years old
He could plan the crops and plant like a grown man,
But there never was enough; his father wasn't thrifty.
And Francey turned drover. In the summer he drove
Beef cattle from Landon Hill to Glens Falls for market,
Walking both ways the thirty-one miles and back,
Taking it slow. He knew cattle couldn't be hurried,
And they had to drink and graze along the way.
He delivered all of them in good shape, the dry cows,
The steers and yearlings—all those that farmers
In his part of the country wanted to sell.
And after he collected the prices he walked back
To Landon Hill. This went on all summer.
I asked him, "Don't you get tired and hungry?"
"Yes," he said, "but I'm paid for driving.
I can put something in my pocket
And at Chestertown I buy some Jackson Balls.
They keep them at Remington's store.
I keep one in my mouth when I'm walking
And let it dissolve. I can tell the miles
Just by Jackson Balls. I know how many it takes
To get me to Glens Falls and how many back,
Not many going back because I'm not driving
And go faster." Did you ever see a Jackson Ball?
They were round balls of hard candy—
Peppermint balls striped with red and so hard
They would last a long time on the tongue.
I never drive over Landon Hill Road
But what I see the shabby twelve-year-old
Keeping the cattle in line for his long walk,
And remember those Jackson Balls—a few pennies' worth
That kept him going on the road
And his measuring the miles by their lasting.

Wax-on-Snow

To a child living in a log house, on a back road, in the Essex County town of Minerva, late in the past century, Christmas was not the most enchanting time of the year. Christmas impressed me, as a child, as a day father did not work: the day he popped corn and cracked nuts, and remained in the house and talked with mother, and when we had a special cake with our supper. For some reason, Christmas trees in the house were unknown. We never had one until many years afterward when we moved into the village of Chestertown. The only doll I ever had up to the time we left the log house was a rag doll named Peggy.

Sometimes, even before Christmas, the roads were blocked with drifts, and father made the three-mile trip to Olmstedville on snowshoes. One winter, I remember, we never saw another woman for three months. We had homemade things for Christmas: new mittens, home-knit stockings, and sometimes a pet from the woods. One particular winter father brought me a *flying squirrel* for Christmas, in a stoppered log. He made a wooden cage for the squirrel, and I had the beautiful little animal for a time. But even the ample supply of nuts did not reconcile the little flyer of the deep woods. One night he gnawed the bars of the cage and fled.

We were the only American family, that is, the only family with early American ancestors in the little farming settlement of houses. The others were French (France-French) and Canadians (Canadian-French) and Protestant Irish from the north of Ireland. None of these families ever had a Christmas tree; I never saw one until I was five years old, when, the weather being moderate, father drove me in the cutter out to the Methodist Church in Olmstedville. Father was superintendent of the Methodist Sunday School; so he was called to sit in a special place while I was left with small children on the center aisle. I was overcome by the tree blazing with snowy candles; toys I had never seen; candy canes and little net bags of candy and nuts. The doll-angel at the top of the tree held my eyes. To me she was *real,* and I gazed at her with awe and delight.

The gifts were distributed, but I hardly saw them—I was looking so longingly, lovingly at the doll-angel. Finally a young woman with a soft voice came to the pew where I sat with other small girls. She gave each one of us a little bag filled with sticks of striped candy and "mottoes," those almost forgotten flat pieces of candy that bore a motto. Mine, for I could read even then, said—at least one of them did—"I love you," and my receiving the little net bag out of nowhere was to me a miracle. There was nothing else for me; but to my childish heart that was enough. I did not see another Christmas tree for several years.

But Christmas was not the time of year that *thrilled me.* When the sun was rising higher in the skies and noonday warmth could be felt even in our frigid backland of country, when the warmth was sufficient to melt the snow from the great yellow birch logs in the dooryard so that I could peel away the curling yellow strips to play with, I waited for the morning when, after prayers, father paused a minute before going outside and said, *"Mother, I think I'll begin tapping today."* Nearly always mother would demur, and my father would say, "Yes, I think I can begin. I want to get the first run of sap; it is sweeter, and, if we can get the sugar to town first, we get a better price." If the snow was not too deep, I tramped through the snow with father.

He tapped with an old-fashioned bit and auger and then drove in the spout for the sap. The spouts had been made of sumac with the pithy center scraped out and shaped at one end to fit his auger hole in the tree. The sap buckets were wooden, and father hung them on the spout or set them under it so that the sap fell into the bucket. From previous knowledge—I was eight years old then—I knew which trees had very sweet sap and those that gave sap that had very little sweetness. Father told me not to disturb the buckets of the very sweet trees by drinking the sap. In two or three days, if the weather favored, the fine hard sugar maples were all tapped, and the fire was started under the great iron kettle that was hung near the camp. The pile of logs to keep the kettle boiling had been stacked near the big kettle the year before so that the boiling down of the sap could proceed without delay. At this point my father's brother sometimes came to help him so that the boiling could continue nights as well as days. The high point for me and for my young cousin, a year less my age, was a "Hallo, hallo!" from the woods that reached the house when father was about to "sugar-off."

We each snatched a tin basin and a fork from the pantry, bundled up, and started for the camp. Near the big kettle we stopped and packed our basins with clean snow. We were about to have that magnificent luxury of early days in the Adirondacks, *"wax-on-snow."* Using a small ladle, father trickled the hot syrup over the snow-basins. It set immediately into the most delectable semi-soft maple-wax delicacy ever tasted. We were not restricted; we could have fresh snow and a second basin. Even Rover the dog, who liked maple-wax, had a twist of the delicacy-wax, which promptly clamped his jaws together until it melted in his mouth.

After the wax-on-snow we went back to the house, and father poured the soft sugar, when ready, into gray crockery jars and the syrup into fruit jars and the few tin cans that were obtainable. This sugaring off went on every few days until the season ended. Father sold the first run and the middle runs of the trees, and we kept the last run for home consumption. I do not remember seeing much white granulated sugar as a child. We made brown bread with maple sugar; cakes, cookies, and doughnuts.

The descendants of those sugar-maple trees still grow where their ancestor trees grew, but no one taps them in the spring now; and only by scraping could one locate the ash pit of old fires that boiled down the sap. What became of the huge kettle I do not know, but it has not been there for many, many years. The house has been taken down, and but for the fact that the side of the mountain is all state land, the summer camp and the motel would now have invaded the old sugar camp. Rover has long since joined canine fellows in a dogs' Nirvana, but the memory of the sugar maples lives in my mind. And in dreams sometimes I hear the *"Hallo, hallo!"* sounding to tell me that sugaring-off is about to take place.

1965

Small sawmill powered by a mountain stream.

Many settlers found the Adirondacks' unique combination of rivers, lakes, and forests advantageous in dealing with the harsh mountain environment. Water was plentiful, since the mountains were not only the main watershed for the state but one of the most important in the eastern United States. Many of the streams and tributaries of the river systems provided enough power for the settlers to mill their own timber as they cleared their land. Since they cleared large parcels of land, ample wood was available for building and fuel.

23

Old Man Wamsley

I never knew that he had a first name.
He had come to the wilderness long ago
In my grandfather's time from famine in Ireland
And settled with the Protestant Irish on the long
Windy hill that looked up to Marcy and Whiteface.
Like the other Ulster Irishmen who came over
In the early days, he wrung a living from the land
In happiness because they had land. He was stiff,
Unbending, savage of temper, ignoring
His two daughters but idolizing the son Wullie
Who went in the lumberwoods winters
And saved his pay for the father.

His house had no furnishings—
None that you could speak of,
No blinds, no curtains, a bare floor,
A sheet-iron stove, a few wooden chairs.
When the neighborhood women offered to make curtains
Before his wife faded away from her hard life,
He refused. "Windows are to let in the light.
I don't want lace hung there to dull the light.
And I want to look out on whatever's around."

He had built a high fence around his orchard,
And although we traded fruit in the settlement
Old Man Wamsley never offered to trade.
He had the largest Seckel pear tree I ever saw,
And in the fall I was hungry for those small
Sweet pears. I would take a small tin pail
And go to the gate of the orchard fence.
The old man would come out roaring at me.
What did I think, that he would give away his pears?
I would listen while he raved at children in general
And turn to go down the hill. Always the gate would open
And the old man would pull me into the orchard,
And still growling, fill my small pail
And give me a pat on the head
And push me out and lock the gate.

Once when I was five I had to go through
The blinding snow the eighth of a mile through the field
To try to get Wullie to come and take care of our stock.
Mother wrapped me and said, "You must get through!"
Blown down by the wind, creeping along, fighting the storm,
I reached the line fence and lay down to rest.
I was sleepy but I knew that was dangerous.

I crawled through with the last of childish strength
And fought my way to the house. I knocked at the door.
The old man picked me up in his arms and carried me
To the stove. He was tender and his voice shook.
"Wullie, Wullie!" he said. "The child out in this storm."
He asked me, "What happens at your house?" I told him.
"Sure," he said, "Wullie will go down."
He rubbed my hands and chafed my small legs,
And held me in his arms to the warmth of the stove.
"Wullie, carry this child down pic-a-back.
And do anything you can for the mother.
It's a wild night for a grown man to be going about."

Wullie rode me sitting astride his shoulders
Down to our log house. The storm was fierce,
But pride warmed me against the cold.
I had not failed my mother; I had fought my way
Up the long hill, and Wullie was bringing me home.

Jane Wamsley, daughter of "Old Man Wamsley"

Large families were important to settlers in the Adirondacks. Typically, the value of the labor supplied by family members was more important than money. Male children worked the farm before, grown up, they left home to earn their own way. Females, on the other hand, knew that if they did not marry or teach school or "hire out," they would become little better than servants in the homes of relatives. Consequently, many left the region to seek employment in the factories and mills to the south and east, while still others went to Boston or New York to become governesses for wealthy families.[64] Tintype courtesy of Mary Whittemore ("Old Man Wamsley's" great-granddaughter)

Wullie

"Put those wet snowshoes in the shed. Breakfast
Is ready. Did you watch by him all night?
It's lucky I told Jane if he was worse
To lift the lamp three times and you would come.
How is he?"

             "Gone—just as the sun came up.
The doctor didn't get there, for the roads
Are drifted with the snow. If he had come
I don't think he'd have kept the old man there."

"And Wullie . . . he's up lumbering on The Gore?"
"Yes. If we could have gotten word to Wullie
I think that would have held him back awhile.
Jane didn't count, but Wullie was his life.
There's something women hardly understand
That a man feels deep down about his son.
He'd deeded him the farm, made sure his blood
Would never come to want. Wullie would have
One hundred acres of fine timber land
And sixty cleared for pasture and for crops.
The old man paid for it by lumbering
When he came over in famine time."

"While his wife lived, I thought that I would give
Her fixings for the house; it was so bare.
But he said, 'No, plain boards are good enough.
We don't want carpet, or curtains.
The windows are to let the light shine in.'
Was there no word for Jane? She's tended him
And been a faithful daughter all these years."
"He hardly spoke of her; Wullie was on his tongue
The whole night long, though Jane sat by his side.
When morning came, we thought he was at peace,
When suddenly he moved and spoke again,
His voice as strong as it was in his prime.

    Wullie's the b'y . . . my Wullie, he's the b'y;
    He bought kerosene oil at the Corners
    For nineteen cints the gallon, Wullie did.

"He settled back and hardly breathed again.
Before we covered him, it seemed a smile
Came on his face, as if Wullie had come."

Mis' Cole

She came walking up the road one morning
In late summer, slowly, taking her time.
She had on a blue calico wrapper,
Which was all the clothes I knew her to have.
Her face was still young, and her hair was tied back
With a leather thong cut from a tanned hide.
I called her in and made a cup of tea.
Then I asked her if anyone was sick.

"No," she said, "they're well. I'm leaving George.
I'm just walking away. Haying is done;
They can't say I left when the work was heavy.
Sarah is fourteen and Luddy twelve.
The twins are ten and Georgie is seven.
They can get along. I'm not coming back."
"Why, Mis' Cole," I said, "Don't say that. You know
You've got a man and five healthy children."

"I haven't got a single thing," she replied.
"Not even a hair ribbon, only leather
To tie my hair. I never have a cent.
Children are children; they have their own things.
I'm only hands and feet for George,
Someone to put the food on the table,
Someone to have more children for him,
And mend and hand-sew their dresses on them
Until they wear out in rags.
I'm walking to Pottersville this morning.
Then I don't know where I'll go; there must be
Better things than I've had in my life, somewhere.
I hope I'll find them. If they look for me
Tell the folks I'll never come back."

I went into the spare room and found
A blue hair ribbon. She took the leather thong
Off her hair and tied on the ribbon.
"It's the first one I've ever had,"
She said. "I'm beholden to you."
I packed a paper sack of victuals for her.
"Don't forget, you'll get hungry," I said.
"I'd hardly feel it, now I'm free, but I thank you.
If you ever find me, keep my secret.
They won't miss me, with the farm work,
And all the stock, and the trout brook,
And the beaver meadows, and the mountain.

"I was an orphan when I married George.
I never had no one or nobody, not even myself.
I have to find someone or something."
She went out, and I watched while she walked
Up the long Wilson Hill.

                             I heard where she was
Down below, but I said nothing.
George and the children got on all right.
It's long ago, but I think of her
And the leather strip in her yellow hair.

O. D. Putnam

A portrait of a woman in a basque dress sitting against a background of cleared land.

While most men farmed and lumbered, women worked as wives and mothers caring for their families. Their long days were filled with endless rounds of cooking and baking, sewing and washing, spinning and weaving. Most of the clothes, blankets, carpets, and curtains were made in the home. During the growing season, the women helped care for the family garden, "putting by" vegetables and fruit against the long winter months. And finally, when men went off to the lumber shanties in winter, women tended the livestock and the fires as well. Some women were teachers in outlying schools but only until they married. Others hired out to cook or sew.[65]

The Mooneys

I saw them every Sunday when we drove to church,
Beyond the schoolhouse, up the slanting hill
Beside the creek, and then a level space
Before you saw the house set to the right
Back from the road in the lush meadow grass.
And every Sunday she was sitting there
Dressed in a decent faded basque and skirt
With her hands folded in her ample lap.
And on the other side of the scant porch,
In checkered shirt thrown open at the throat,
Bill Mooney sat with pipe between his teeth
And chair tipped back to balance with his weight.
Every Sunday from late spring to fall, they sat there
Like two stones, or like two trees rooted in earth.

"Father," I said, "do they not go to church?"
"They're Catholics," father said beneath his breath.
"But don't they drive to Mass with their own kind?"
"No," father said. "The priest comes here to see them.
French Louis says they will not go to church;
They do not want to leave the house for fear
It might burn down, or cattle should get out,
Or other damage come. They go to town sometimes
On Saturday nights and bargain for their groceries
At the store. Folks say they're surely touched.
French Louis knows them better than I do.
He says they came from Ireland years ago
When there was famine. For a while they worked
In logging camps, or anywhere, and saved
Enough to buy their farm; then land was cheap.
They kept on working till they built a house;
The neighbors made a bee to raise their barn.

"I've asked the Mooneys if they wouldn't come
And visit us out on our farm someday.
They said, 'I know you'll think we are queer folks.
We feel sometimes that we are deep in sin;
We're happy to stay home, sit on the stoop,
And look out on our fields of oats and rye
And watch the cows down in the pasture lot,
And sheep and the young lambs up on the hill.
It's strange to you who never wanted land
To call your own that we are filled with fear
That some old spell might sweep it all away.
Sometimes I take a sod the plow has turned
And hold it in my hands and think of years
When not a cackling hen or bit of turf
Could be our very own.

'We know it's wrong—
To never leave our land and cows and sheep
To kneel in church—but still we say our prayers
And ask God to forgive us for our fault.
We feel that surely He will understand.'"

Local taxidermist.

Settlers depended on fish, game, wild berries, and nuts to supplement what they harvested from their land. In addition to meat, vegetables, fruit, and other food staples, they raised sheep for wool and grew flax to spin and weave for clothing.[66] They gathered sumac and butternuts to dye carpets and blankets, tallow and bees' wax for candles. They saved fat for soap and plucked geese for feather beds and pillows.[67]

Creeping Charley

I think you must have seen it by the road
Or covering the yard of an old house
Where folks have nailed the blinds on all
The windows, and gone away, and for some reason
Never come back—and all the flowers have died,
And the hop vines grown over last year's vines.
Then "Creeping Charley" spreads out everywhere
And creeps and creeps—the grass can't fight with it—
And fills the yard. It's such a pretty sight:
The faint green leaves with edges silver-white.
It has another name I've heard it called:
"Snow on the Mountain," and it looks like that
If you should see it covering a slope.

It runs all over the old Bennett place
Now Charley's gone: I always think of him
A-creeping round and spreading quiet-like
Just like the plant. He was a kind of stranger,
Although he'd always lived here in this house.
And all his folks had lived and died here too.
We never played with him at school, not much;
That is, we never felt he had the knack for play.
And somehow he grew used to looking on,
And when he was a man, 'twas just the same
At caucus, or town meeting, or at church.
But he was always where the others were.
He never failed to be down at the store
On every evening when the men sat there,
A-blinking with white eyelashes. After a while,
Someone threw out after him the name
We knew him by, when he'd slunk away like smoke,
Without a word. "There 'Creeping Charley' goes,"
One said, and after that he had that name
And never any other while he lived.

I don't know anything he ever did
That one could speak of; what was bad
I'm sure he never thought of in his life.
I don't know what he thought of as he sat
Always a-listening, always creeping round.
He never talked, and if you spoke to him
'Twas "Mebbe" and "Likely," " 'Pears so" and "Well, well."
The weather never tempted him to say
Aye, yes, or no. If you went past his house
He'd never call you in, but stand and look.
He was just there like stumps and old gnarled trees

Not worth the cutting. All his life we thought
That we should never miss him when he went.
How can you miss a thing you've never known?

We looked at him; perhaps he looked at us.
But if he knew us and saw differences
We never knew; none of us found out
What he was like in all his sixty years.
He was just something there, a sort of thing
That made no sound, took nothing, no, nor asked
Anything of us. He was much too scared
Ever to look a woman in the eyes.
I never heard one ever looked at him.
He went on working on his scrubby farm
And selling stock and saving what he got.

Now that he's gone it's queer that some of us
Find that we miss him more than other folks
Who made some stir. He left his farm and cash
To the church fund to help out needy folks.
His house is nailed up; everything runs wild;
The yard is just filled up with that green plant
That we thought he was like. Why some folks
Pass through this world, I never could make out.
They're "Creeping Charley" souls, but I suppose
They have their uses. I remember now
Some folks called that plant by another name,
"Snow on the Mountain," and it may be now
Someone has found another name for him.

The William and Joanna Lavery home, one mile west of Olmstedville, Town of Minerva, Essex County, New York. Far left: son, William; third from left, Aunt Joanna.

Frame houses gradually replaced log structures, and wood stoves became the main source for heating and cooking. Most of these frame houses had three chimneys, two in the main section of the structure and one in the shed or summer kitchen.

The house was built as close to the water supply as possible, ideally with a spring in the cellar to facilitate fetching water for the family. If a spring or brook was not available, a well was dug and stoned up. Water was kept in barrels in the kitchen pantry.[68]

Antiques

"Come in, Mis' Pasco. It's a hard long climb
To get up here; I used to ask Pa why
With all the farms down toward Athol way
He bought this one up where they say 'two stones
Grow to one dirt.' It's hard to work a farm
When your plow turns up more stones than soil.
I'll put your things in the best room and make
A cup of tea; this April air is chill.

"Here's sugar, but I think you take it plain
Just as I do. When you are warm we'll talk.
I know you want to hear just what I sold
To that young man who drove up here last week
Hunting for old things on these country roads.

"Well, first he tried to buy that old cord bed
With posts that Grandpa carved of maple wood.
Why land, Mis' Pasco, I told him—that bed
We sleep on now—I couldn't part with that.
Besides, it has a history; my children came
On that old bed, and others before mine.
Besides, there's nothing half so comfortable
For sleep and rest as a fine old cord bed.

"He wanted all my haircloth parlor set
And that stand with the marble top I used
To hold the lamp beside my spare-room bed.
The stereoscope and my old pewter mugs.
Why land, Mis' Pasco, I'd be living here
In a bare old house if I had let him take
The things he craved.

                              "Then he went upstairs.
He almost talked me down to get the swifts
And spinning wheel. I said I still spin yarn
And I shall use that wheel while I'm alive.
I keep the carpet loom in the north ell;
He wanted that and all the yards I wove
To give the children—old rag carpeting.

"When we came downstairs he saw my old steelyards
Hanging on the wall and grabbed them up.
'Those you can't have,' I said. 'Why all my life
I've weighed butter that we sold and meal
With those old steelyards. One side will weigh out
To fifteen pounds, but turn it over, then

37

It weighs to fifty; we weighed all the wool
And maple sugar; it's like an old friend.'

"Even my small tin skimmer caught his eye.
I told him money wouldn't buy my things
That I had lived with all my life and used.
They're friends. We'll get along some way.
The taxes aren't too much here on this hill."

"You say you didn't let him have a thing?"
"That's fine, Mis' Pasco. Come in the best room.
I've lighted kindling in the stove; it's warm.
We'll have our tea in there and take a look
At my new pictures for the stereoscope."

As time went on I took three counties over,
Essex and Warren . . .

When Jeanne Robert Foster was seven her parents moved to Chestertown in Warren County where her father again lumbered and worked as a carpenter with his brother, Will. Her family lived in a number of places in and around Chestertown: first with her father's brother, who lived on Pine Street; then on the Foster farm, owned by the parents of the man who would later become her husband; and finally in the old Braley home adjacent to the Fosters, the oldest house in the village.

The move from the isolated farm to the village brought Jeanne in contact with a different life. She was soon attuned to the religious, social, and political interaction of the community, and the effects it had on its residents. The Chestertown map helps to illustrate her long prose article about the village.

My First Journey

My first journey, taken at the youthful age of seven, was incident to the removal of our family from a secluded country farm to a small town some fifteen miles distant.[69] Our starting point was a rudely built log house set in the bend of a peaceful river that wound its way through a narrow, elliptical valley rimmed on every side by low-lying mountains. Between this log house, which had been our home, and a tall well-sweep that rose nearby from a tangle of lilacs stood my father's stout farm horses, harnessed to a wagon bearing a huge rack upon which were heaped, in wild confusion, our humble household goods: stoves, chairs, tables, beds, pots, pans; and crowning the grotesque pile, our sole claim to gentility, an ancient carved mahogany chest of drawers bequeathed to us by my great aunt Polly. There I was upon my airy perch, for I had begged to ride to our destination upon the load of furniture with my father, rather than in the more comfortable buggy which conveyed my mother and sisters to the new home awaiting us. After a final survey to see that nothing had been forgotten, my father mounted the board seat at the front of the rack, clucked to the horses, and with a great creaking of ropes and clattering of pots and pans we were off on our own wonderful journey.

Slowly we climbed out of the valley, up, up, following the grass-grown, uneven road through a notch in the mountains: then down in a gentle descent of perhaps more than a mile to the ford. Here the river, tumbling out of the valley, widened out to flow in shallow, dancing ripples around a verdure-clad island, whereon grew in profusion spikes of some beautiful scarlet flowers. As the horses paused to refresh themselves with a draught of the cool water, I reached down and plucked my father's sleeve.

"Father, father," I entreated, "do gather me one of those pretty flowers."

My father looked at the depth of the water, which was over the hubs of the wagon wheels, and answered kindly, "No, little daughter, I should get very wet. Besides, they are but wild flowers after all."

I said no more, but my eyes followed the gay blossoms after we climbed out of the ford, until a bend in the road bore them from my view. Never in all my life had I wanted anything more than I desired one of those nodding crimson flowers. Soon, however, my childish grief was allayed by the varied scenes each turn of the road brought to my curious eyes.

There were prim farm houses among fruit trees, their windows screened with hollyhocks and morning-glories; a red windmill with flapping arms; a weather-beaten schoolhouse where a group of children played a merry game at their recess; and at the crossroads, when some five miles of our journey had been covered, an open black-smith shop from whose cavernous depths a shower of sparks leaped to the rhythmic sound of the hammer upon the anvil. I was properly terrified by the appearance at the door of the smith himself, and I fancied one of the goblins had come to life from out of my fairy tales.

Beyond the smithy our slow and tedious progress led past a quaint stone lime-kiln crumbling away from disuse; and farther on, a tiny white church crowned with a square belfry, through whose broken shutters I could discern a brass bell. After a few more miles, I fell sleep from sheer weariness of sightseeing; and when I awakened it was twilight, the wonderful amethyst twilight of the mountains, and the evening star shone faintly in the sky above the heads of our horses.

I plucked my father's sleeve again. "Father, are we almost there?" I asked.

"Only two miles more, little daughter," he replied, and then bade me wrap myself well with a blanket against the chill of the evening air. Soothed by the added warmth of the blanket, I fell asleep once more; when I again awakened we were halted in what appeared to be a vast amphitheatre of light, so brilliantly did the illumination from half a dozen oil street lamps and several well-lighted buildings dazzle my eyes.

I crawled out of my blanket to the edge of Great Aunt Polly's chest of drawers and stared down into what I afterward knew to be the village square. Several men were standing about in the slouching attitudes of village ne'er-do-wells; three boys chased each other about the square in a game of leap-frog, shouting and laughing as they jumped; and from the outer darkness, beyond the circle of the flare of the lights, came the flash and flutter of the light garments of a woman. Then my father came to the side of the load, apparently from nowhere.

"We are home, little daughter," he said. "Look up and you'll see the telegraph wires I've told you about times enough."

I looked up and perceived, crossing and recrossing against the stars now fully out in the heavens, a dozen or more black wires. A thrill ran through all my being. These were the mysterious things that my father had told me girdled the earth, everywhere carrying power and dominion. As my father lifted me down from the load, the realization came for the first time that I, little unknown country maid of dolls and pinafores, was a part of the "whole," a part of this same "power and dominion," and I was ecstatically happy.

1909

O. D. Putnam

Village of Chestertown, Warren County, New York.

As pioneers from New York, Vermont, Maine, New Hampshire, Connecticut, and Rhode Island started across the country after the American Revolution, many stayed in the Chester area. The Schroon River was on the east, the Hudson River on the west, and the old military road led to the Lake Ontario region.

The navigable section of these rivers had long been used for transportation. There logs were lashed together into large rafts and moved down stream. Norman and Alanson Fox were the first to float single logs down the mountain sections of these rivers. They would stack logs on the banks of the river until the spring run-off would provide the water and force to carry the logs downstream. Lumbering became the economic base for Chestertown. The tanning industry soon followed with hides being imported from South America, Spain, and Australia.[70]

CHESTERTOWN

Tn OF CHESTER
Scale 20 Rods to the inch

CHESTER

POND

TANNERY

G.Mill

Mrs.Pasco

M.D.Knapp

Chester Tannery

R. Braley

J.H.Faxon

M.D.Knapp

D.H. Gould

J.Braley

R.J.Thurman Furniture Shop D.H.Gould

J.Braley

A.S. Pasco

Wagon Shop

H.C.Remington

C.J.H.Faxon

C.H.Faxon

G.F.Bryant (oc)

Mrs.Dimi.

Wood & Wather

A.Sherman

O.Collins

E.B. Smith

N.B.Mallory Store

Frances Barrett

Tripp & Loy Store

PRES.B.CH.

J.Bronson Pastor

Res.Bronson

J.Remington

C.H. Faxon

LeClaire

S. Tabor

Bowyer

Wm Scofield

W.Wickham

B.S.Sh.

C.J.Noxon

C.J.

M.Tripp

&

C.J.Loy

Bro. Pickett Store

Dr.E. Magee

N.E.Ch.

Mrs.H.M. Eaton

C.Prouty

J.Stone

Store & P.O.

M.D.Knapp

C.H. Faxon Res.

Braley & Johnston (oc) Store

Miss E.Noxon

U. Young

M.E.CH. Parsonage

M.H.Downs CHESTER HOTEL

J.Armstrong

C.Sh.

G.F.M.

J.Pierce

C.Fowler Res.

C.F.

Mrs.M. Blanchard

H. Young

C.F.

R. Mead

BAP.CH.

SCHOOL N.2

A. Tabor

W. Wickham

Cab.Sh.

H.Kittenbeck

J. Remington

C.Fowler

B.S. Warren

H. Thompson

J.B.Braley

P. Gould

E. Warren

MAIN ST.

Map of Chestertown, from *County Atlas of Warren, New York, 1876*, printed by
F. W. Beers and Co., New York, N.Y.

The Old Village

This story is easy to understand, easy to see in the mind's eye. Once upon a time there was a quiet village in the foothills of certain western mountains of the northern Atlantic states. It was built around a crossroads, and at the crossing of the white, dusty dirt roads were the main store and the butcher shop, the harnessmaker's, and the hardware store. A little farther down the main street were the shoemaker, the tinsmith, the drugstore, and the schoolhouse. And ringing these around with dignity were five churches.

There were the cream-colored Methodist; the very white Presbyterian spire; the humble little Catholic in gray under its lifted cross; the darker gray Episcopalian that had a touch of Gothic and was timber up to the gables of the roof inside; and the shabby Baptist nearby that once had been white but was weathered and stained and grown with moss. There were only a few Baptists and they were poor. Indeed it was rumored that one wealthy member of the congregation owned the church itself, having bid on it to save the edifice from sale by foreclosure of a mortgage. Large elms and maples cast their shade around these buildings and ran out in stately rows down the Main Street and the crossroad, which was called West Street.

Down Main Street to the south were the furniture shop and the Odd Fellows hall over Moffat's shop. Moffat was a handy carpenter who did odd jobs. When the Odd Fellows were not using the hall, the Good Templars had their meetings there; and both societies had gay suppers and even a masquerade now and then.

Below the Moffat shop lived M. the local liveryman. He was a large man who drove to the fairs and on Sunday afternoons, with great dignity on these occasions, in a shiny-topped buggy. He sat behind a pair of handsome dapple grays with long sweeping tails and full manes and flicked a shiny whip over their ears. He wore on these occasions a long gray coat and a dun-colored top hat that must have been his father's. At the livery stable just behind the hotel, fat in his shirt sleeves held up by blue elastic bands, with twinkling eyes and a long reddish beard, he eternally washed wagons and hitched up "rigs" and cautioned amateur drivers and gave advice to farmers on horse diseases, and told stories and chewed tobacco. He had a son who drove out with the colts on a road cart or sulky of the old high-wheeled variety to break them in. It was supposed that Bertie had inherited without study, with his facial characteristics, the vast knowledge of horseflesh possessed by his father. He was a boy set apart and regarded with certain awe by the young fry. And he was silent like his father. He never talked of his horses or of his exploits at the local fairs when he was sometimes permitted to drive in the free-for-all race.

Below the Moffats lived the harnessmaker. He was a Scotsman who had found his way to that country so like his native heath in youth and had fastened himself into the village life. His work had become a legend in his lifetime. Old farmers would display a set of horse collars and say Sandy McTavish made them, that they would last forever, that there was no better collarmaker.

Below these dwellings of those who served stretched a street of houses built on the old colonial lines with gracious dignity of ample cornices or lintels and paneled doors; white houses, spic and span, with green blinds. Almost at the end of the street where the white road skirted a low meadow where violets grew in late spring, and curled around a hill covered with young pines, was the "oldest house." This house was gray as weathered wood could be; low roofed, with a backward-slanting wing the full length of the house, and a low veranda. The walls inside the veranda were plastered, which gave a curious gleaming quality to the house at dusk or even at night. Inside this house were heavily beamed rooms; two fireplaces, one with a brick oven; and a long, low attic where one could see the holes for the guns of the pioneers, closed since Indians no longer threatened. And downstairs off the "best room" was the room where, you were told in a hushed voice, the man was chained who danced himself to death.

And below this house was "the last house" in the village, southerly. The name "the last house" had set it apart for years and lent a dignity. This house had a white picket fence around the dooryard, whiter than the house itself, and a board walk from the picket gates to the doors. A tall locust tree shaded the front rooms, and a crabapple brushed the side windows. Maples were set outside the fence, and a long row ran down the road and half concealed the red barn that was connected with the house by a covered runway. Beyond the trees spread the expanse of "the pasture" where the village cows shared scantily or abundantly according to the rains and the season. Occasionally the calm of the mornings and the tall hollyhocks in the dooryards were disturbed by the rattle of wheels of a smart buggy; or a phaeton with a canopy top; or by the jolt of lumber wagons or hay ricks; or by the plod, plod of oxen and the "Gee-Haws" of the ox drivers. And in the season of the county fairs there was much dust from people from "below" ("below" meant from any town or city southerly) driving to the fairs, and an unwanted smell of cigar smoke from the cigars of those city dwellers who came to try ancient and dusty bunco games on the natives.

So much for Main Street southerly. Northerly it stretched up onto a hill covered with cedars and bore on each side houses of gentle dignity and families of tradition and repute. Westerly the crossroad that came in from the east carried the second section of the village.

Here the two local doctors hung out inviting shingles. And here the French blacksmith, another wanderer from Canada, had built himself a house and a shop; the house with "dem dormer windows" he so much admired, and the shop very low and dark and wholly unventilated except by the door, which always framed a shower of flying sparks from his anvil. There were more of the white houses with green blinds, and then came the curve of the road that led to Cork and the tannery.

Now Cork was the result of the tannery. The tannery was a beautiful, long, red building with large windows that framed lithe-muscled men scraping hides. Behind the building were piles of hides that sent out a malodorous smell, and great piles of fragrant hemlock bark used in tanning. Below the tannery the water dripping from the dam and flowing through the sluice glittered and danced in the sun. Above the level of the tannery itself were the dam and the tannery pond and Cork.

The great man of the village kept a tight fist on his pocketbook. He had built houses for the tannery workers of pine boards, two rows of ugly boxes that were the forerunners of the ugliness of the modern average country house, and had painted them with yellow priming paint. Their lines were not bad, through no virtue of his intention but because his builder did not quite know how to frame an ugly house; but their miserable dirt yards, their lack of gardens, their uncurtained unwashed windows gave the ten or twelve houses a forlorn air. They were clearly outsiders. And when the local great man brought Irish immigrants to the country town to scrape the hides and tan them, the double row of yellow houses was named "Cork." And long after the tannery had become a trousers factory with the onward march of progress, and long after the old building lay empty, crumbling in decay, with the water flowing uninterrupted over the low dam from the pond beyond, the name "Cork" clung to the place.

Nobody from Cork went to the village churches, except perhaps to a surreptitious mass at the dove-gray Catholic church; nobody who lived in Cork ever was recognized as a part of the village. Such was the snobbishness of the old town. Little girls from the best families and the second-best and third-best families carried their skates on their arms through Cork in the winter to go skating on the pond beyond, walking with haughty head turning neither to right nor to left. Nobody knew the names of the families who lived in Cork. One was not supposed to know. In the snobbish little self-contained village, it simply wasn't done. I never knew the name of a family who lived there. I vaguely remember that latterly an itinerant shoemaker named Smith crept into the place and rented one of the houses from the great man; and that certain economical and thrifty souls sneaked over to the yellow house to have taps put on by the cobbler because his prices were lower than those of the established and respectable vendor of leather on the Main Street. Between Cork and the village was the grist mill.

There was an old miller as well as a young apprentice miller. I remember the thrill of approval that fluttered over me when the apprentice miller, a boy of perhaps eighteen, came to the door of the mill to bring my father a sack of meal or of buckwheat flour, white flour caught in his blond hair and sifting over his ruddy face and fringing the long light lashes that lifted over dark blue eyes. He was a fair-haired boy of the town's old English blood, blood that still produced the finely modeled Saxon face; even in the meanest of the village folk, one saw a trace of an old culture. They were quiet and smiling, undemonstrative and peaceful; but when the guns fired on Fort Sumter they went out by twos and threes and by dozens, and only a few came back, a few that in my time straggled up the street as the "Grand Army of the Republic" on Decoration Days, one solitary Zouave among them, in incongruous red and baggy trousers.

The village had three stocks: these English who had built the village; a few assimilated French-Canadians; and a few assimilated Irish. These last two were in the minority, about two percent of the population. Sundays all the churches had a fair quota of worshipers. They came from the town and from the countryside. Practically everybody went to church. The best families, who made annual pilgrimages "down below," came in cashmere, the girls in thin white, with slippers and tiny parasols. The second-best families came in wool or muslin as the season varied; the third-best in ancient raiment well preserved, a wedding dress or some festival attire of long ago; the outcast remainder ventured into the sacred edifices in humble calico.

There were the village characters. First, the great man who had all the lumber on the hills and owned the tannery and the row of houses called "Cork." His house was the great house in the middle of the town, facing the inn. Few of the villagers had ever seen its august interior. From a glimpse that I had one time when the door was inadvertently left open, I know that there were large flowered carpets, and walnut furniture, and marble-topped tables, and wax flowers under glass domes, and a damp musty smell, and long Nottingham lace curtains. The great man drove out every afternoon behind a beautiful span of bay horses. He was driven by his man, a combination clerk and valet. He was the only man who had what he called an office in the town, a low white building connected with his house by a walk that ran along the back of the lawn by the row of hollyhocks. One never saw the great man's wife except on Sundays and special occasions. She stayed somewhere in the depths of the damp and gloom in the great man's house.

Then there was the other rich man. He lived on the westerly street in a long white house with terraces that fell away down to the sleepy stream called "the Creek" that was the outlet of the Tannery Pond. He was retired; and as he was silent the young fry never knew what he had been. One heard that he had had "lumber," but to us that was indefinite. We saw him as the primrose on the river's rim; he was Alexander Remington and nothing more. We were far more interested in the two medicos.

One was a pudgy medico who had the confidence of the countryside; and the other was the tall, lean medico with the English face and the air of distinction who had the confidence of the village. It imparted an air of elegance to have him seen entering one's house. I remember going after him—a great adventure for he lived at the hotel—in the dead of night when my father was taken with a sudden seizure. He walked down the snowy street with me under the bright wintery moon, his long arm bent to hold my short one, the mere effort of half lifting me drawing me close to his side. I forgot all about father. I wanted to walk on forever. Indeed, so strong was the spell that I sometimes dream I am walking along that star-bright path in the snow of February with the dark mountains on either side. He smelled faintly of cologne and pungently of drugs, and strange smells filtered between the two. I saw that his face was serene.

There were the village butcher, the storekeepers, the withered druggist who dragged one foot, the changing clergymen and their families, the village good-for-nothing, the wild young man, the wild young girl over whom the elderly women shook their doleful heads; the church charge, a forlorn old maid who lived a lugubrious existence by boarding around with the Methodist flock and sewing for her keep. There was the lady of the old family who went out to work. She was a sacred institution. Her husband's lack of judgment had forced her to undertake papering for the community, and cleaning—not washing, which was beneath her dignity and skill. She was an artist in homemaking and housekeeping. All I know of those arts she taught me, with many other things. She was a born berrypicker. Don't skin, she would say. Pick the big ones. Let the other folks pick the little ones. If I have succeeded at all it is partly because of habits Mary Poulder inculcated in me before the age of twelve.

But one might go on endlessly about the village characters; there is a novel in each one; laughter and tears, and the hush of strange reverence. It is the life of the village that I want to give you, a life as fresh and vital as the buoyant young pines that lifted from the hills; as delightful as the flavor of spicy mountain fruit.

First there was the life of the village as a religious community, the communal entities existing side by side and interpenetrating, known as the Episcopalian, Methodist, Baptist, Presbyterian, and Catholic churches. There was the extra social life of the village in which the churches, with the exception of the Catholics, mingled. There was the trade life, a pleasant stir and bustle in the streets, a trade life that held the community of the locality for a radius of ten miles 'round about the village. There was bartering of wood and hides, hemlock bark and grain, potatoes, corn, butter, eggs, honey, and what not; or in winter, skins of foxes and mink. There was the life of the school, an intense, pulsating life that the children knew vividly, their elders faintly. There were the doings of the Odd Fellows and their ladies, of the Good Templars. There was a singing society or school that met twice a week and every night before concerts; there were really good voices in that school, too. And there was a dramatic society that gave two evenings of plays in the ballroom of the old hotel, or latterly in the town hall over the principal store, and also one minstrel show in winter.

There was the village band, a good band with two sets of instruments, best and second-best; and long red coats, and white horse tails for their helmets, and gold braid and fringe at the shoulders. They had a little band house down by the creek where the members practiced nights. Village wives were in the habit of speaking of the band as wives now speak of the club: its attractions were the menace of their evenings at home. The bandhouse was always the retreat of the henpecked husband. And there was the baseball team. That was the pride of the village. Its team was almost always the champion of the countryside for a radius of fifty miles. They went abroad in neat gray uniforms with the name of the village in red letters on the chests of the suits and nearly always carried the gray and maroon to victory, as they did when some other team invaded the home grounds. If one could not keep a baseball score, one did not speak of it.

And in addition to this activity, there were those that came to us from the outside world. We were greatly agog when the presiding elder preached in the village church; once even a bishop had honored the village. There was a one-ring circus that came and pitched a tent opposite the schoolhouse and stretched a slack wire from the shop to the schoolhouse and sent a nimble clown in sparkling tights and trunks to walk up and down above our gaping mouths. There was *Uncle Tom's Cabin*, which came every summer and played in a tent below the Catholic Church. There was a street parade before the performance, with the trusty bloodhounds held in leash by Simon Legree in moustaches and long boots. There were the dark, melancholy Cassy, Emily, Eliza St. Clair, and the heavenly little Eva, the last riding in a white cart behind a Shetland pony; and there was the beloved Uncle Tom.

There was the pleasant stir of local politics in the autumn: the rivalry between the Democrats hopelessly in the minority and the Republicans triumphantly in the majority. The Democratic meeting place of political cronies was the blacksmith shop; of the Republicans, the general store. And after the elections, with what awe did we youngsters gaze at the successful candidates. No maharaja inspired more respect than the newly elected supervisor; and the butcher, a man to be hallooed on sight because a fearsome figure, once he was invested with the dignity of the office of sheriff. I myself never dared address the stumpy, lean clerk of the great man who carried the slight honor of justice of the peace. And into the sharp rivalry of local politics came the distant reverberations of federal politics. These indeed disturbed the village slightly; they voted largely as the fathers did before them, solidly on party lines. The Prohibitionists who subscribed to the prohibition paper *The Voice* with its motto "Vox populi, vox recti, vox omnipotens" were the insurgents. But then evil drink did not disturb Main Street, except on a Saturday night when the stage driver and the Irish vat tender at the tannery might celebrate by an unsteadiness about nine o'clock and a none-too-particular salutation under the kerosene street lamps.

No one had heard of Karl Marx. There was no Carnegie Library. The libraries of the Sunday schools sufficed for the reading public. These contained *Barriers Burned Away, The Opening of a Chestnut Burr, He Fell in Love with His Wife, Last Days of Pompeii, Little Women*. In the last days of my stay in the village, I remember, a fierce controversy was waged within the dovecote of the Episcopal Church over Geikie's *Life of Christ*. This questionable book (according to the most orthodox) had been brought to the village by a young priest who had browsed on the higher criticism at the theological seminary. But the storm passed. Geikie was forgotten, and the disciplined, sad-eyed young man, went back to the safety of Canon Farrar. He was never trusted by the elders of the church during his stay in the village, on account of Geikie and because of his once or twice, before he was apprised of his misconduct by his elders, having appeared in his shirt sleeves and played ball with boys in front of the parsonage. In the village the priest was a man who lived by supernatural powers. I felt that it was somehow a mistake that he found it necessary to eat. At donation parties I always stared at him as he swallowed hot oyster stew and pork and beans and frosted cake and pickles, and I wondered if those ordinary and familiar viands fed the grace of God and the powers of the Holy Ghost. After admonition from the elders as to the etiquette of village rectors, he appeared in the morning and afternoon alike in a long black coat, called in the village a Prince Albert, and a very shiny top hat. Clad thus correctly, his appearance gave a thrill to the pastoral call. One received him as one received an angelic visitor; one listened to the counsel of one indeed set apart for the service of God.

The passage of the seasons in the village had a charm that I never have found elsewhere. Winter was perhaps loveliest. The mountains covered with firs that caught the snow and flared it in ferny crest to the sun made the mornings and evenings like mountains of brilliants. The thaws driving the melted snows into the swollen creek backed the waters over the low meadows until shallow lakes surrounded the town, and froze, and made joy for the skaters. And the snows were never blackened by smoke or grime; they covered us with whiteness sometimes from November to late April. We could depend on sleighing. Everyone had sleigh bells, large and small. There were gay cutters, but best of all were the bobsleds that brought the wood and the hay over the snow roads.

Spring was slow with us, a delicate, faint spring.

1924

51

O. D. Putnam

The Oliver children. Left: Clara, Frances, and Julia [Jeanne Robert Foster].

When I was young I overheard Mrs. Wyatt Mead say to my mother, "Mrs. Oliver, it IS a pity your oldest child is so homely. There's not much chance in the world for a girl like that." My father commented, "Well, she can always be a *hired girl*. People still want good cooks and hired girls up here in the Adirondacks." I peered into my mother's bedroom mirror and asked myself, "It's true . . . what *can* I do?" The story of what I DID would make a book.[71]

The Romany Sign

Gypsies came when berries were red
On the twigs of our old thorn tree;
They hung a kettle and cooked a stew
That tasted good to me.
I was invited when gypsies came
And camped on our meadow land,
For mother gave them her good white bread
And whatever we had on hand.
The men had silver hoops in their ears,
And the gypsy queen was gay
In all the colors of Joseph's coat;
And I wanted to run away
And ride in the covered wagon
Where the gypsy children rode,
With a scarlet kerchief on my head,
And start when the sunrise glowed.

But the gypsy queen said, "*No, my child.*
We have camped on your grassy land
And you have brought the gypsies food,
So we love you and understand.
You must return to your home tonight;
But still we will make you ours.
I will set a sign on your forehead now
That gives you a gypsy's powers.
The *Romany Sign*—[she crossed my brow]—
You will carry until you die;
You will never be content away
From the hills and the open sky.
You will sing the songs of the open road
That we lilt in the gypsy tongue,
And set your feet to far-off shores
With a heart forever young.
Your blood will leap when you shall hear
On your road, a gypsy strain;
It will set your feet to the open road
And far-off shores again."

The gypsies were gone in the morning—
Only the wind knew where—
Leaving the red on the thorn tree,*
And an unseen trail in the air.
But their spell was strong upon me;
And always my heart goes free,

*Original line: And the berries on the thorn tree,

53

And my feet obey the *Romany Sign*
That the gypsies set on me.

A true story of the time when I was
ten years old, when the gypsies camped
on our farm in Chestertown, N.Y.

Blue Calico: The Ingrate

Esther Mead always wore blue calico,
The dark-blue cheap kind printed with white sprigs
Of running white vines scattered over it.
Folks liked it to piece into bed quilts
For it didn't fade and made nice dark blocks.
Esther Mead wore it summer and winter
Because she never had anything else,
Except a gray alpaca a church member
Had given her to wear for best Sundays.
She was a frail old maid; her eyes seemed
Full of tears even when her lips smiled at you.
She took care of her folks until they died.
There was nothing left when the bills were paid;
Then she was too old to hire out to work;
So the church members took turns boarding her
To keep her away from the County House.

My neighbor came to see me one morning
When I was putting Christmas things away.
She was excited; her eyes were snapping.
"I want to tell you about Esther Mead,"
She said. "I've always thought she was thankful
To church folks for her keep the year 'round,
But she's turned out ungrateful. She told me
That she don't want that good blue calico
Cyrus Brown, the store keeper, gave her
For Christmas; he's been giving it to her
For ten years.

                    "We church members boarded her
Year in and year out. She was always welcome,
And nothing was asked of her except mending
And doing the starched washing and ironing,
And, come fall, the pickling and the canning;
She always seamed my pillow slips and sheets
And did plain sewing—but what's that? Nothing
When she had her food and a place to sleep.

"I don't remember she said a thank you
Last year for my old gray alpaca dress
I gave her to wear to preaching service.
Now she says, 'I don't want that *blue calico:*
I've sewed it and worn it all these years.
I've always got blue calico on the Christmas tree—
Never anything else . . . but this year.
There was a box tied up with ribbon bows,

With a bottle of real perfume. I heard
The new schoolteacher hung it on the tree . . .
Sweet like musk roses. Then I remembered
The musk roses growing in our dooryard
When I was small, and a dress I had then,
Real silk and shiny and the color
Of the roses . . . Take the calico back
To the storekeeper. . . . I don't want it.'

"That shows she's an ingrate; we could send her
Down to the County House; she's a pauper.
When I told the storekeeper what she said
He asked me if she was in her right mind.
Then when I told him about the perfume,
He asked me, 'What on earth would Esther Mead
Do with a scent bottle? I don't have them
In my store. I'll say that she's *ungrateful*.
I've put ten yards of fine blue calico
On the Christmas tree for her every year.
I'm glad I could see my way to afford it.'

"Would you believe it, just now when I left her,
Instead of getting at the starched ironing,
She's sitting by the sink doing nothing,—
Crying with the tears rolling down her cheeks—
And smelling of that bottle of perfume."

Mary Gould, Professional Berry Picker

Yes, there are some wild berries hereabout,
But you have to know where to find them.
This town was built on a kind of sand plain,
And some things don't grow well here, timothy
And wild berries; strawberries like it least;
And if you want to go picking wild berries
You have to know where to find them.

I *do* know, for I had a great teacher.
We called Mary Gould a professional
Because she could always find the wild berries.
As far as I know, I was the only one
She took along when going berrying.
(I've tried to take her place berry picking.
She's been gone now five years strawberry time.)
There weren't enough berries for all the folks,
And so Mary kept folks in the dark about places
She found them.

                I hear they're setting out plants
In gardens now, and it won't be too long
Before everybody can have berries.
That's why I'm telling you Mary's secrets.
Mary went out working—sometimes for pay,
But mostly just to help folks in trouble.
I helped her when she came down to our house
When mother was sick; I was fourteen,
And one day Mary said to me, "I'll take you
Berrying with me tomorrow." My heart beat fast
For she never took anyone berrying.
"I'll be waiting outside at five o'clock.
You'll get wet, for the dew's heavy that hour."

We went through the red gate into the pasture
And climbed the steep hill and walked through the woods
Into a meadow where the soil was rich
And wild strawberries grew.

"By nine o'clock," she said, "there might be five people
Here berrying, for this is the only field
Within miles where you can pick strawberries.
Don't pick the stems—just the ripe berries
For they're so scarce we must leave green ones growing.
By the time the other pickers come, we'll be home
Will full pails. Careful, don't trample the grass down.
This is a hayfield, mind where you step.
This grass is timothy, and wild strawberries
And timothy like to grow together."

We were home before other folks thought of going.
We had walked a full five miles.
Our skirts were dripping but our pails were full.
"Mind you don't say a word and I'll take you again."

We went out for red raspberries down the Schroon River
Or miles away toward Friends Lake.
Mary taught me how to layer my berries
With raspberry leaves so they would not crush
On the walk home, and to bring two pails,
And take care to pick only prime berries,
And to walk carefully on the way home
So they wouldn't mash and get juicy.
We walked five miles to get blackberries,
Five miles to the Amasa Mead farm.
She had done him a favor, and she was the only one
Allowed to pick blackberries in his pasture.
We walked fast and got to the farm
Just as Amasa turned his cows into the pasture.
"I'll leave the bull in the yard till you finish,"
He said. "He might take a notion to be mean.
Come to the house when you finish so I can let him out."

We went into the pasture; there were islands of small trees
And brush; the blackberries grew on these islands,
Long sweet juicy blackberries. Mary canned them
For the church fair and always took first prize.
"I'll teach you here on this first tangle where they grow.
First look and see if they're thick or if they're been
Skinned off. Folks do get in here when Amasa's away.
If they're thick, pick only the big ones.
We'll skin the field that way.
And if we don't have enough we'll come back around
And pick the small ones. If they're not thick on the bushes,
Pick every one that's ripe. And go fast;
We want to be out of here before the sun is high.
Put blackberry leaves between layers of berries;
We have a long way to walk home.
And cover your pails with big leaves.
When we strike the main road folks will be looking
To see what we've got and where we picked them.
Not many will walk five miles—ten up here and back—
But you can drive up here.

                    "We'll give the sick
Some of all we pick any time of year, and jelly.
I'll teach you how to make raspberry jelly,
And the best raspberry pie you ever ate."

The Dancing Man[72]

You take a chance up here in the mountains
Moving into an old house. Sometimes folks
Who lived there before don't want to leave it,
Even though they aren't on earth any more.
I'm sorry you bought the old Daly place
Without asking the neighbors about it.
The Daly house is the oldest in town;
It was built before the Revolution.
The big corner timbers and hand-hewn beams
Have kept it standing. In the loft, folks say,
There used to be vents in the timbering,
For muskets. They're boarded over now.

Neighbors could have told you about noises—
A tap-tapping you hear in the east room.
We say the noise is Hezzie Daly dancing—
Leastwise his ghost. He was kept in that room.
You'll notice the plank floor is worn down thin.
He was odd and queer when he was a boy,
Kept to himself and never said too much,
But always went to church and read the Bible
And sat under preaching as if he had
Some private understanding with his God.
One Sunday after he heard a sermon
On King David dancing before the Ark
With shouting and with psalteries and harps,
Hezzie started dancing on the way home
And never stopped as long as he had life.
He hardly slept; nothing could quiet him;
He said he was praising God by dancing.

He danced until his bones showed through his skin;
Sometimes he danced at night out on the road.
Finally his folks had the blacksmith come
And build a cage to keep him in the house
In the east room—the marks are on the floor.
He's been gone years and years, but those who lived
In the old Daly house heard him dance nights;
Leastways they thought the noise was Hezzie's ghost
Tap-tapping, still his way of praising God.

If I were you I'd buy some lumber now
And lay down a new floor in the east room.

The Old Pine Tree

Trees are just trees now; we take care of them
For what they are—their use in the future,
Their beauty, and their right to keep growing.
But in the North Woods a long time ago
Certain trees were folks; people went to see them
As great persons in the neighborhood. It seemed
They gave counsel with leaves and needles
And bark that the mountain folks understood.
There was the Lavery silver-maple tree
That grew by the corner of the old house
Where the bright hollyhocks grew in summer.
Folks came from "down below" to visit
And hear the wind ruffle its silver leaves
And feel a kind of peace that sifted down
Into the heart after you sat in its shade.

There was a giant elm on Landon Hill.
A praying family tended the tree,
And when folks came to see it they'd have prayers
Under its shade . . . It had a kind of soul.
Folks came to sit under it—stopping by
As if it had a special blessing in its leaves.

But the old tree best loved in the North Woods
Was the Old Pine Tree below Chestertown
Opposite the baseball diamond.
Half of the roots clung in the hogs-bank
Of sand that used to shadow the old road.
The other half hung naked in the shade,
So large, so old they were a gallery
For all the tired when the baseball nine
Played Schroon or any other North Woods town.
Folks loved that tree, and in the year of the great
Blizzard men shoveled all day long to reach it.

One day a man came up the Warrensburg Road
With the news that the Old Pine Tree was gone.
A man from out of town who owned the bank
Of sand had cut it down the day before.
It had some "market logs." He needed the cash.
The Old Pine Tree; it was incredible
It should not be there; children and grown folks
Grieved for that tree and touched the drying stump.
More than three score of years have passed,
Yet the old folks passing the place
Will say the Old Pine Tree stood there.

As time went on I took three counties over,
Essex and Warren and Wild Hamilton, . . .

Jeanne Robert Foster's family sent her south of Chestertown to live with various relatives when she was young. From 1887 to 1889, for example, she stayed with the Francis Putnam family in Johnsburg, Warren County. Even though the Putnam boys, Osmond David and Elliot, were much older than Jeanne, she developed a close and lasting relationship with them as well as with their sister, Mary, who was a year younger than she. Osmond often took Jeanne with him when he went around the countryside with his camera, earning money for seminary. His pictures, most of which are printed for the first time in this book, add a startling realism to Jeanne's poems. An early map of the Town of Johnsburg shows the land that she loved and knew intimately—its mountains, rivers, and lakes.

During the winter of 1889–90, Jeanne lived in North River with her uncle, Jacob Davis, a peddler. With him, she traveled frequently to Blue Mountain Lake in Hamilton County, helping to care for the team of horses. The following year she stayed with another uncle, Erastus Griffin, on the Lake Pleasant Road near the tannery town of Griffin, which was located on the banks of the Sacandaga River.

From eight to twelve, Jeanne struggled side by side with the men and women of her mountains to survive the harsh environment. It was probably during this time that she found the strength and independence that would later take her far beyond the Adirondacks.

Johnsburg Corners, Warren County, New York.

Many settlers were lured to Johnsburg with a promise of an industrial settlement from power supplied from Mill Creek. The economy flourished with the development of a saw mill, grist mill, store, and distillery. There was also a woolen factory and one of the first calico-printing mills in America. These industries created a demand for grain, flax, cord wood, and farm products that brought other settlers to the area.[73]

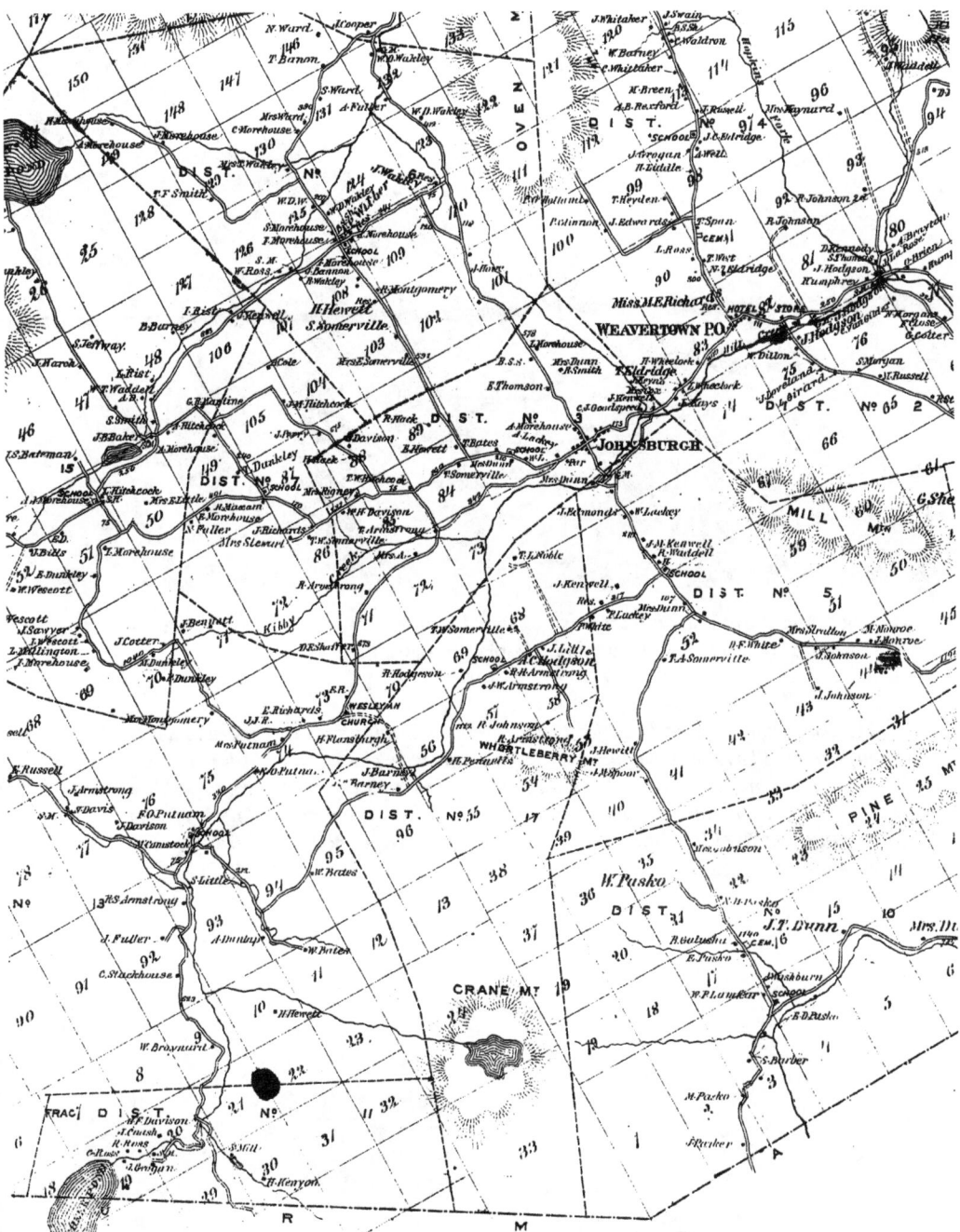

Detail, *County Atlas of Warren, New York, 1876*, printed by F. W. Beers and Co., New York, N.Y.

Log house above Putnam Farm near Crane Mountain, Town of Johnsburg, Warren County, New York. The family is probably the Bates family.

The pioneering families who settled in the Adirondacks understood that it would not be an easy life. The rugged mountain terrain was carved by glaciers that left boulders and rubble and sandy soil, often only an inch in depth, on a base of hard, granitic bedrock. Winters were long and harsh with penetrating cold and yearly accumulations of snow ranging from 90 to 165 inches. In many regions there were fewer than 100 frost-free days a year.

The Lost Breed

You may find traces of them on the land,
If you know where to look and your heart is there,
Or your people lie in an almost forgotten
Burying ground, circled with white pine
That now knows no fear of the lumberman's ax.

There are hollows that once were cellars.
You will know them by the blue columbine
That grows with catnip and stinging nettles,
Or by the white musk, loved in old gardens,
Or by a tame apple tree of good fruit
Mixed in with the wild ones that were not grafted.
And in the fields there are lines of grasses
And wild flowers that grew under rail fences.
Here and there a tree has survived, the black locust,
The silver maple in a wild second growth.

In Chestertown the old pine tree is gone
That shaded the children and the crowd
Watching the games of baseball long ago.
The Faxon empire is no more—today
They do not know where Frank Potter kept shop
And kept the Faxon empire from crumbling.
Milo Knapp, second in lumber building,
Sleeps unremembered high on the hill.
No one remembers the Joe Barton place
On the road to Kenyontown, the old sitting room
And parlor looking down toward the sawmills,
The mammoth grapevine and butternut trees.
All are gone. No one asks for Sam Pasco
Or Jim Scripture or Kenyontown.

Keep on the road when you have broken over
The hill to Johnsburg. The log houses have left
No trace between Centerbar's and the Putnam farm
Lying beside the steep side of Crane Mountain.
The barn is standing, but the house is down.
It was a gracious house with bird's-eye maple woodwork.
From this house Francis Putnam
Went out preaching Sundays to Bakers Mills
And gave his time to funerals and the sick.
His land was a part of the Putnam empire
Shaped by his worldly brother Enos
Out of the farms on Mill Creek Road. His hills
Flowed with cattle and sheep and horses.
Behind the house was the nursery land

Where he grew fruit trees for sale: the Gill Flower
Spice Sweetings, and the new Russian apples.

It has all gone, the district schoolhouses,
The Georgian churches. Men no longer
Come home in spring from logging,
Or draw bark in winter for the tanneries.

Enos Putnam and his wife, Sybil Daly Putnam

Enos Putnam (1810–65) and his wife Sybil (1804–85) were one of the early families who lived in Johnsburg. Enos, a descendant of Israel Putnam, the Revolutionary War hero, became a Methodist minister after his wife, a former school teacher who came from Connecticut, had taught him to read and write. The Putnams had six children: Henry (adopted), Francis, Mary, Sara, Martha, and Enos. Henry was killed in the Civil War. Francis became a minister, and Enos became a wealthy farmer in Johnsburg. When their children were grown they adopted Lucia Newell, renamed Eliza (Lizzy) Putnam, after her father had drowned in the Hudson River while driving logs downstream and her mother could no longer provide for her. Lucia Newell was Jeanne Robert Foster's mother.[74] Photographs courtesy of Paul Schaefer.

Wesleyan Methodist Church

The Wesleyan Methodist Church on Mill Creek Road was built by Rev. Enos Putnam in 1859. He was one of the dedicated group of Methodist ministers who, at the Syracuse Conference in 1848, seceded from the Methodist Episcopal Church because the parent body refused to condemn slavery. Known as a fiery abolitionist, Rev. Putnam helped move escaped slaves through the mountains and into Canada. The old log house adjacent to the parsonage was the Johnsburg station of the "underground railway." From there Rev. Putnam would move slaves on to the next station.[75] Photograph courtesy of Paul Schaefer.

The Old Church

Yes, I reckon the old church will fall down.
It's more than a hundred years old.
There's only one man in the township now,
Ike Kenwil, who remembers the man
Who was the first preacher. I talked with him
The other day; he's ninety. He told the story
And said somebody ought to set it down in writing.

Up on the Putnam farm there was a red house.
York brown, we called it; the paint was outcrop.
All you had to do was to go up on Crane Mountain
And get you a bucket or two of red soil,
And when you mixed it with oil, there was York brown,
Sort of reddish and it lasted forever.
Well, just east of the red house was a log cabin,
One where the preacher lived when he built the church.
It was logs but it had a deep cellar. That's where
He hid the slaves until the night
He could carry them on to the next Underground.
He had the cellar all comfortable and a stove down there
To keep them warm if they ran away in winter.
He was one of the old Putnam breed, Enos Putnam.

The preacher's wife, so Ike told me, came from down below.
She was a smart schoolteacher.
Enos was a farm boy who couldn't read or write,
But he fell in love and he got the town clerk
To write his love letters; so they got married.
She said, "I love you and I'll teach you;
You shall be a minister." And after a few years
He got enough education to be ordained.
Neighbors helped him; he built the old church
Nigh ready to fall down that stands at the crossroads,
Georgian steeple and all the old horse sheds.
Ike remembers the preacher was a fierce abolitionist.
They called him "nigger preacher"; cat-called him at town meeting.

Well, the war came on when they fired on Fort Sumter.
And the preacher's boy Henry volunteered.
He used to write home about singing in the trenches,
'We'll Be Gay and Happy Still"; Ike remembers best
The cold January of 1863 when the preacher held a meeting
In the church; his loyal members helped him bore holes
In boards to set tallow candles in the long windows.
The congregation met. The church blazed.
The preacher read the Declaration of Independence

And the mighty words of our rail-splitter president
That freed all slaves forever and ever.
And as he was reading, a man opened the door
And came running up the aisle with a paper.
"For the preacher," he said, and the preacher opened it.
His hands shook but he read it out to us.
"We inform you that your son, Henry Putnam, was killed . . ."
Ike said tears ran down the preacher's cheeks,
But he held out his hands in benediction.
"The Lord giveth and the Lord taketh away."

It's quiet around the old church now.
The old preacher and his sons and grandsons sleep there,
And Sybil, the schoolteacher who taught her husband to read
And made him a preacher; the grave stones lean away
From the wind. Some of them are sinking down.
Soon they'll be covered and folks won't remember.
When I go there in winter a few withered flower stalks
Bend in the wind above the graves. The wind shakes the steeple.
Soon only the soil will remember that this church
Was an outpost of freedom. Mice scamper up the aisles.
The pulpit chairs are ragged, the pews are musty.
The door isn't locked; nobody cares, you can walk inside.
When I do it's a fancy of mine that I hear voices.

O. D. Putnam

The Enos and Sybil Putnam House, Mill Creek Road (Garnet Lake Road), Johnsburg, Warren County, New York.

To the left of the Putnam's red frame house stood the old log cabin where Enos Putnam met runaway slaves at night. For a period after her husband's death and while her adopted daughter Lizzy was still in her teens, Sybil Putnam lived with her son Francis and his growing family; later she returned to her own home. After Lizzy's marriage to Frank Oliver she would often come to stay with her mother during the long winter months when her husband was away in lumber camps. It was during March of 1879 that Jeanne Robert Foster was born in the house painted "York brown" from pigment found in the stream bed between Whortleberry (Huckleberry) and Crane Mountain.[76]

Shadbush

In May I climbed Crane Mountain
To the timberline's high edge
To see the shadbush blooming
Below each rocky ledge.

Then I climbed again for berries
That ripen there in June.
Clusters of crimson fruiting
Follow the early bloom.

There is no savor like them
As they crush upon my tongue.
They carry a magic with them,
And my heart is ever young.

Love came when the shadbush blossomed,
Love I still recall—
When the petals stir in springtime—
That did not meet the fall.

Let a shadbush mark my sleeping.
I may find love again
In a dream of one brief springtime—
Its glory and not its pain.

O. D. Putnam

The Rev. Francis Putnam Farm at the base of Crane Mountain, Town of Johnsburg, Warren County, New York.

That I lived in more places in the Adirondacks than my family did was due to the fact that I was parked out with relatives from eight until the spring when I was twelve. This in turn was due to several facts: my absence meant one less mouth to feed, and we were very poor.

Also, for two years my father's young brother Eugene lived with us in Chestertown. My father nursed him, as did my mother, until he passed on of pulmonary tuberculosis at the age of twenty-five. He used two rooms of the house kept closed against the children for fear of infection. My absence was planned because he [was feverish and] wanted to be fanned. He had books; we had only three. So I sneaked into his rooms whenever I could, and while I fanned he allowed me to read Southey, Moore, and Browning.

From eight to ten I lived at the foot of Crane Mountain with the Francis Putnams. Here I earned my first cash by guiding parties up and on Crane Mountain. I received 25 cents every time a tourist party came asking for a guide. I also knew where the cave at the foot of the mountain was, and other items of interest: yellow orchids, the amethyst quartz bed, the garnet outcrop.[77]

The Francis Putnam Family. Left: son, Elliot; wife, Julia; daughter, Mary; father Francis; and son, Osmond David.

Francis Putnam (1836–97) was a kind and gentle man who, like his father before him, entered the ministry. Francis moved his family to Crane Mountain in mid-winter and built a crude cabin in which to live until spring came and the land could be cleared. With the help of his sons he constructed the farmhouse, barn, carriage house, shop, and sugar house. Shortly after the house was completed, Francis took in Jeanne Robert Foster to live with his family, just as he had done years earlier with Jeanne's mother, Lizzy Putnam. Elliot (1867–1941) became a minister and returned from Readsboro, Vermont, to farm the family's lands after his father's death. Osmond David (1861–1926), a skilled photographer, left the ministry and became a farmer and carpenter in Wilton, New York. Mary, a year younger than Jeanne, married and moved to Schenectady with her husband.[78]

Minister of the Gospel

Si Putnam was a minister of the gospel.
When he was young he used to go out on charges.
He was an ordained minister and went to conference
Every year, even when he was old.
But now that he was old, he worked his farm
And preached over at the Mills where folks were too poor
To have a regular preacher. He didn't get much money
And never anything for weddings or funerals,
But he really didn't want anything. He would have preached
Anyway, and worked his farm to get his living.

I lived with his folks a while when I was growing.
He would write a sermon every week and I would read it
Aloud to him on Saturday night after chores were done.
He preached over at the Mills schoolhouse every Sunday.

One week when he was just plumb tired
He didn't write one, and he called to me.
"You go upstairs and put your hand in the barrel
In the hall by the desk and pull out a sermon.
Reach deep down and get an old one.
I've been preaching so many years round the circuits,
There'll be some there that're new to folks
Here at the Mills."

                  I went upstairs and reached down
Into the barrel and pulled out a paper,
Folded, tied with a cord, and marked "sermon."
I gave it to him. He unfolded it and put on his glasses.
"You'll have to go up and get another," he said.
"This one's on hell fire and damnation.
Folks hereabout are having such a hard time this winter
To get a living, what with taxes and all,
I don't like to preach on hell fire and damnation."
I went back and pulled another paper out of the barrel.

"This one's all right," he said after he'd looked at it.
"I preached this one up at Chazy on 'saving grace.'
You be ready and we'll start about eight tomorrow.
It's ten miles and the roads are drifted."

"Maybe," he said, as he righted up the cutter
After the brown mare had floundered in a snowdrift,
"Maybe folks won't turn out, account of the weather.
If they don't, it's all right, I won't blame them.
But a minister of the gospel has to keep his appointments."

There was smoke coming from the chimney of the schoolhouse,
And there were cutters and blanketed horses under the shed.
The congregation was standing around the stove
When we went in, trying to coax green wood
To heat up the old sheet-iron stove.
He greeted each one—Sister Galusha, Brother Richards.
He shook hands with everyone and inquired after their health
And patted the children who had come out with their folks.
After the wood burned up a little, he stood in behind
The teacher's desk and said, "We'll start the meeting.
Brother Watson, will you raise the hymn?
We'll sing 'Woodworth Long Meter.'"

Brother Watson raised up his lean, scraggy six-foot-four
And set the tuning fork against his teeth to get the key.
Then he lifted the tune:

> Just as I am, without one plea
> But that Thy blood was shed for me,
> And that Thou bid'st me come to Thee,
> O Lamb of God, I come, I come.

They sang the six verses; the air in the schoolhouse
Seemed warmer. Outside the wind screeched, the snow furled.
The minister preached the old sermon on saving grace.
Gradually something shone out on the weatherbeaten faces.

John Centerbar

"Make some hot tea, mother, and set out milk.
John Centerbar is coming down the hill
With the jumper. Pity he's never had
A shod sled in all his life, or bobsleds.
It looks as if he has all his children."
Father put on a warm coat and went out.
John drove his horse into the yard.
He was part Indian and part French
And lived in a windy house on the hill.
"Top of the World" we called it; he could look
East into Thurman and west into our township.
John got out of the jumper and came in.

The cold was bitter; he was glad to be warmed.
A kind of wagon box was rigged on the jumper.
It was full of skins of animals, mostly hides,
And an old quilt or two. The heads came popping up;
John had his five children in the jumper;
He was taking them seven miles to the Corners.
My father called them into the warm kitchen;
They came running—barefoot in zero weather.
John couldn't take them out in summertime;
He had no wagon. It was a treat for them
To go to the store at the Corners
And maybe have a stick of peppermint candy
If the storekeeper felt generous; he knew
The hunting had to be good to have soup
Where John Centerbar lived.

                            The children had
Black straight hair and brown stained faces. Their eyes
Were like bright black beads with a spark
Of sharp light in them. Mother gave them milk;
Then they climbed back into the jumper.
John stayed on in the kitchen a minute.
Father said, "John, you ought to be ashamed;
I know you haven't got the money for shoes,
But you could have me write to the poormaster.
They'll freeze their feet."

                            John pulled at his shaggy beard.
"I know you mean well, neighbor, but I won't be
Beholden even to the poormaster.
Skin'll grow on cheaper than leather."

He got into the jumper, clucked to the shaggy horse,
And went over the hill to get to the road
That went to the Corners.

O. D. Putnam

Enos Putnam and his three children, Kate, George, and Martha (standing).

Enos Putnam (1835–1912), strong in stature and authoritarian by nature, took over the Putnam family lands and managed a prosperous farm on Mill Creek Road. He extended his holdings, accumulating great wealth in property and livestock. His first wife, Margaret Little (1834–86), came from Ireland and was well educated: she taught her husband and attended to business matters, as well as to caring for their three children. George (1861–1931) continued to farm the land after his father's death. Martha (1867–1971) taught in district schools and graduated from Albany Normal School; she returned to Johnsburg to marry Noble Armstrong, a neighbor along Mill Creek Road. Kate (dates uncertain) married her brother-in-law's cousin and lived in the immediate area.[79]

Ben Enoch's Cowbells

Folks on mountain farms loved to hear cowbells.
If you've ever heard them you remember
The bells ding-donging faint and far away.
Ben Enoch didn't have an ear for music;
He never sang the hymns in church on Sundays,
But he had a good ear for his cowbells.

Ben lived on a wild farm near Crane Mountain,
And his cows were always straying away
Into the woods beyond the hill pasture;
So he strapped bells on all his cows and heifers,
Big bells, little bells, any kind of bell;
And when the cows didn't come home for milking
He'd listen, and he could tell right where they were
The minute he could hear a bell ding-dong.

I was at his home one day when the cows
Were late. Ben said, "I'll listen for the bells.
They're ringing now; that jangling bell you hear
Is Daisy, the lead cow; she's out roaming.
The sharp bell you're hearing would be Maggie;
She had her first calf this year, she's looking
To find it, but it's not in the pasture.
Her bell tells me she's down in the fallow.
I must put a poke on her tomorrow.
Maggie's smart; she can dig my potatoes
With a forefoot; she jumps my log fences.

"That sweet bell . . . that's Jenny, my young heifer;
She's on the ridge coming down the trail.
I know where they are when I hear the bells."

I thought, as I listened to the jangling,
That Ben Enoch had some kind of ear for music;
He might have carried the hymn tunes on Sundays
If they had been played on cowbells.

Horse-powered fanning mill for buckwheat at Hank Hewitt's log barn, Town of Johnsburg, Warren County, New York.

During haying and harvesting, men gathered from neighboring farms to help one another and to share equipment. They grew barley, oats, buckwheat, corn, and potatoes. They planted apple orchards and tapped maple trees. Once crops were in and homes made ready for the long winter months, many men left their farms to work in lumber camps in order to provide for their families.[80]

Second Wind

Some folks have curious things tucked away
In their minds, lying around in corners.
Now there was Milo Brown; he had something,
And I should have found out about it when
He was on earth. He called it "second wind,"
But there was more to it than the name,
Something we didn't rightly understand.

I found out about it one haying time
When Milo Brown came to me for a job.
Mostly we changed works, but I hired Milo,
For he didn't own a farm or a house,
And he had a pack of hungry children.
Milo was little and lean and scrawny;
I wondered if he could keep up mowing,
Swinging a scythe all day in the hayfield.
He said he could, and I let him start work.

We were mowing the north meadow, uphill
Where the timothy was tall with tough stalks.
He started out with us in early morning
And kept his end up until ten o'clock.
Then he sat down on a stump and I thought—
I was right, Milo can't go on mowing.
We all stopped to have a drink of switchel
That my wife had sent out to the mowers.
I said, "Milo, is it too tough for you?"

He did a little sweat-mopping. "It's tough,"
Milo answered, getting up from the stump,
"But I won't know it when I get second wind."

"I've heard say of your second wind, Milo.
Does it always come on time?" I asked him.
"It comes," Milo said, "when I need help
To keep up with other folks; I'm scrawny;
The Lord made me that way, but he helps me;
I found out that when I've used up all my strength,
Then I get my second wind; there's something
Inside me that goes right on with the work
Like a strong man was doing it for me
And saying, 'Milo, just keep on trusting.'
I've trusted; my second wind never failed."

Milo whetted his scythe . . . I like the sound
Of whetstones ringing out in the hayfield . . .

And he went on mowing. He mowed easy,
And when we got to the top of the meadow
Milo was ahead, laying a long swath
Even and straight. He didn't look tired,
And he wasn't as beat as the others
When we went back to the house for supper.
He's gone now, and I wish I had asked him
To tell me more about his "second wind."
I could use it myself many a time.

Shadders

Granny climbed up old Crane Mountain.
Neighbors told her not to go.
"Shadders pick on moonlight evenings;
Shadders watch the berries grow.

"Folks have seen 'em in fog-white moonlight,
Eyes as bright as a bat a-wing;
Hooty-owls calling, moles a-crawling;
We wouldn't go there for anything.

"Better climb the ridge to get blueberries."
Granny lit her pipe again;
Said, "I aim to do my picking
Where they're sweetest, on old Crane.

"Berries sweet as maple sapping,
Berries big as a green wild hop
Grow on the sides of old Crane Mountain;
I aim to climb to the top—tip-top."

Granny clucked, set her pipe a-sparking,
Bright tin bucket flickin' in the sun,
Went on the mountain to pick blueberries,
Rounded a boulder and she was gone.

Didn't come back when night was sifting;
Didn't come back sun-up next day.
Neighbors said—who goes blueberrying
On old Crane has gone to stay.

Folks have seen her climbing with the shadders,
Filling her bucket in fog-white light;
Hooty-owls calling, moles a-crawling;
Picking blueberries on a moonlight night.

O. D. Putnam

The Enos Putnam Farm on Mill Creek Road (Garnet Lake Road), Town of Johnsburg, Warren County, New York.

Enos Putnam's extensive farmlands included frontage along both sides of Mill Creek Road. The well-appointed farmhouse provided very comfortable living quarters for Enos's family. In the smaller building adjoining the main house, Enos ran a store where neighboring families could buy such staples as flour, sugar, tea, and coffee. Across the road, in a maze of buildings, stood a large, multi-level barn for livestock. A wagon ramp provided access to the upper level, where hay and grain were stored.[81]

The Brothers Return

Enos: "Come up in the hill pasture; we can see
Most of my farm and sit down in the shade."

Francis: "I'd like to sit down there and talk awhile
Where the sweet fern grows in the damp gullies.
I remember when I was a small boy
The scent of the trampled fern when the cows
Started coming to the barn for milking
Their hooves sucking the mud from the bottom
In spring; there was no mud in the summer.
The hills were burned to a crisp in August,
The pennyroyal would sift to seed dust
Between our fingers."

Enos: "I don't remember
But the sweet fern made poor milk if the cows
Ate it in with the grass; the high pasture
Always worried me after June; I would
Turn the cows out on the meadow after haying."

Francis: "There are some things you do not remember—
The things that drove us apart when we lived.
Now we can sit down; we are in the shade
Of the beech trees; we can see your great farm.
Look Enos, you can see the churchyard; the church
Is still standing; it needs a coat of paint;
You kept it painted for you always thought
About the outside of things. We can see
The graveyard where we lie; the tall white stone
Is yours, a rough moutain boulder is mine.
The old steeple, square upon square, may fall.
Who cares? Who remembers? No one. Our people
Are gone; that is why we are here today.
Sit down by this rock; it is cooler here.
Now that we have returned, what shall we do?"

Enos: "I know my work. Look down at my great farm.
Where are the buildings, the long barns,
The white house with the picket fence, the trees,
The bee hives set on planking, the cattle,
The sheep on the hills, the cows, the horses?
My fences, my stone walls and the orchards?
The shearers and the threshers, they have gone.
Not one of my three children loved the land.
They finally lost it; the farm died then."

Francis: "What can you do now, Enos?"

Enos: "I must build!"

Francis: "But how? What can you do; the land is waste."

Enos: "I must find a man who still loves the soil
Walk by his side unseen, pour in his mind
What I loved when I lived until he builds,
Sows, reaps, and covers these hill pastures here
With sheep and cattle, mows the meadow land,
Grafts the old orchard, makes it bear again
Knowing that we are lost if the land does not yield."

Francis: "Some one will listen to you; he will feel
Your words within his mind and he will hear
The land speak to him for the soil will speak
If men will listen. I have more to do.

I must go back to our old quarrel again
I stifled in your mind; you were so strong
I had to go into the wilderness
To find my God. I cleared the land and built,
Set orchards growing, plowed and sowed and reaped,
And preached the gospel in our father's church
And in schoolhouses when a few could come.
Kneeling in furrows, I sent up my voice
Until strange things came to me; I felt a power
That lifted me and set things into place.

The bats keep sanctuary in my house;
It lies in ruins; all I built is gone,
But I have greater matters in my mind.
Men stand at a crossroads today; the earth
Spawns evil that arises from old graves.
Storms gather such as we have never seen.
I must go where men gather who would serve
The great high purposes that once we dreamed
In words that shaped a home for liberty,
And shout in soundless words until men find
The nobleness that set us to this land.

We leave each other now. Walk down to the road
With me, for I would take one thing with me—
The scent of sweet fern in the August sun."

The Red Peony

There was a red peony in her yard,
The only flower left; the old beds were grass.
Low rims of turf showed where flowers had been,
Rosemary and white heliotrope,
Sweet cicely, pansies, and bleeding heart.
Now, only the red peony was left
For her to tend and dig about mornings
In the spring when shoots came up like red squill.

When the peony buds came out in late June
She would sit afternoons out on the stoop,
Prim and straight in a high-backed old rocker,
Watching the peony, her silk gown crackling
A little when she moved, her collar tight
At her throat, fastened with a gold brooch
That held a curl of hair set behind glass,
And folded on her shoulders a white scarf
That her grandson had sent her from Java;
The fringe fell over her hands—she liked fringe.

Once when I sat there with her on the stoop
The wind blew peony petals over the grass.
And she said, "I don't want to look ugly.
Will you put my silver combs in my hair
When I blow away, and new white ruchings
In my best black dress, the one I will wear?
I think perhaps you might lay this white shawl
Around my shoulder; the fringe is pretty.
And rose-geranium leaves in my hands."

She looked at the red peony petals—
"The wind's blowing the peony away:
I've watched it year after year budding out
And then blowing away over the grass,
And waited for it to come back in spring. . . .
You'll remember about the silver combs
And the white shawl, the one I'm wearing
With the fringe. I want it over my hands.
If it was only red instead of white,
It would look like my red peony petals."

Rev. Osmond David Putnam (1861–1926)

Rev. Osmond David Putnam took . . . photographs when he was a student at Houghton Wesleyan Seminary and was home for vacations. His negatives have only a range of Warren County and part of Essex County because he walked or took early stage wagons while carrying his camera.

The Boiled Shirt

There was a certain strangeness about folks
Who lived on solitary farms up north long ago.
Sometimes they didn't seem to have much reason
For living at all, life was so bleak.
They had so little and never complained.
There were the Burnhams; they were dirt poor,
Piney and Fred and the two grown boys.
The boys were grown men but they still lived at home.
Sometimes they hired out to work in shanties.
No one ever heard that they were courting.
Their farm was small, a stretch of sandy land,
The hay was mostly wild grass, no timber
Except scrub that made poor wood for the stove.
No farm stock except an old horse and cows and yearlings
That always looked hungry. Even the hens
Were lean from always chasing grasshoppers.

But they got along somehow through the year
Living on what they had and Piney's glory.
Every Sunday at the big camp meeting
Held once a year out beside the Hudson,
After the sermon when the minister
Started exhorting the sinners to repent,
Piney would "get the power" as she called it,
And rise up and scream like a mountain panther,
And sinners would take it as a warning
And come down and kneel at the Mercy Seat.

Their farm was about two miles beyond ours.
One Sunday I went there to take her picture.
Father had given me a camera that summer
To help me earn my keep out at Houghton
Where I was learning to be a preacher.
Piney wanted a picture of the boys
And herself and Fred, for all that she had
Was a tintype taken their wedding day.

Their house looked like some logs piled together.
When you saw smoke and then a window's shine
You knew it was a house where someone lived.
It was dark inside; some of the windows
Had been boarded up to keep out the cold.
There was a cidery sweet smell that came
From strings of dried apples hanging
From the logs, bunches of mint and catnip,
And long ears of corn braided together.

"Piney," I said, "we'll have to go outside.
It's too dark in here to take your picture.
Bring Pa and the boys out into the yard."
As I went out I heard angry voices.

"Pa and the boys are arguing," Piney said.
"Each one of them is bound he'll wear *the shirt*.
We're poor; we never had but one boiled shirt.
I hand stitched it of white cloth; the bosom
Is all little tucks that will hold the starch.
They've always took turns about wearing it,
But today each one wants to wear the shirt.
I said Pa should have the right; all the brunt
Of the hard farm work always fell on him. . . .
Here they come now. I'm glad I've had my way.
Put Pa in front when you take the picture.
You can see that he's wearing *the boiled shirt*."

The Shared Church

"Where's Miss Oliver?" I asked that Sunday.
The August day was hot. "She's walked out
To go to church," her niece said.
"But I thought the Baptists had it today."
"Not if Grandma can walk. Here she comes now.
That's six miles she's walked with
That hot bonnet tied under her chin.
You know the one with the pansies on it."
Grandma climbed the steps and sat down.

She was warm and tired, but her eyes blazed.
"I kept them out. They were there
And going to hold service on our Sunday
And have two Sundays together.
But I sat down in the church as congregation.
And when the time came, I sang the hymns.
When they asked me why they couldn't hold service,
I said this was our Sunday. And even if
The minister was away, that I was congregation,
And I had come to church and it was Methodist Sunday.
They should keep out. They said some mean things
About me and all the Methodists,
But I shut the door on them and knelt
Just as I always do when the minister's there.
I blame him: ministers shouldn't take vacations.
They never did in the old days.
So I walked out and held our Sunday.

"We believe differently. They immerse
And we sprinkle; and there's other differences.
I read my Bible out loud; so if they did wait
And hang around at the door they could hear me.
I read here and there beginning with Jeremiah:
'Stand in the gate of the Lord's house
And proclaim there His words.'

"I've had a long hot walk, but I was doing
My appointed work. And as for them,
If I shouldn't make heaven, and get sent to hell,
The first ones I'll meet there
I know will be the Kenyontown Baptists."

Camp meeting site at the outlet of Mill Creek Pond.

During the summer, many Protestant churches hosted "camp meetings" that lasted about a week and were the highlight of the church's yearly activities. These assemblies were primarily evangelical in nature, where people from neighboring communities gathered to hear guest preachers from the denomination's headquarters. The church served as the social as well as the religious center for its parishioners. In the Johnsburg area, camp meetings were held at Riverside (along the Hudson River) as well as at Mill Creek Pond.[82]

Mountainside Camp Meeting

At every camp meeting there was a service
Part way up the mountain on a bare ledge.
It was held at five o'clock in the morning.
It was called the sunrise meeting for all
Sanctified souls, and the elect and the faithful
Struggled up there to pray just at sunrise
With their ministers.

               It was a fine thing
But hard on the lame and the old
As years went by to go on announcing
Sanctification by their climbing up
To that high perch to meet the Lord at sunrise,
Especially on an empty stomach.
You were supposed to go fasting.
I heard Grandma Oldham talk about it
One morning in her campground cottage.
Grandma was having a hearty breakfast.
She said, "I'm supposed to be sanctified,
But it's curious how unsanctified I feel
After I've climbed on an empty stomach.

"When you're walking 'round the campground
Or sitting listening to the preachers
You're sort of certain of your religion,
And keeping sanctified is quite easy.
But when you've climbed up to sunrise service,
And you breathe hard and your feet are sore,
You forget you're sanctified and you wish
You had a cup of hot tea with sinners
Instead of the prayers with the camp meeting ministers.
And right in the meeting I wasn't praying,
Not about holiness and the Lord.
Would you believe it, I was just thinking
Since it's August and my son has a garden
That he promised to bring me today at the cottage
Some fresh cucumbers.

                   "Now if there's a thing
I'm fond of when fresh garden stuff comes in
It's fresh cucumbers and vinegar. I was thinking
About them. I'm not sure any longer,
But maybe my sanctification's just worn off."

Mis' Bethel

"Who's going to have her house plants?"
"I don't know. She made a sort of will
And said they were for folks who loved
House plants; her niece told me
Neighbors could come and get them any time.
She's keeping fires, you know, in the old house
Until the furniture is all moved out.
There's no one in these days, not even kin,
Who wants to live on that old scraggy hill.
She even burned green wood in her iron stove,
Drying it out a little on the hearth,
And all for sake of house plants that she loved.

"They cut her calla lilies when she went,
And put them in her hands. Why don't you go
And pick out what you want? There's every flower
That could be raised up here in winter time.
There are lots of balsams, white geraniums
And flowering maple, star of Bethlehem,
Fuchsias and pink oxalis, a wax plant,
Madeira vine, and one great sprawling pot
Of Christmas cactus that's in bloom right now
In her south window."

                            "What about her things?"
"They're all bespoke, even her paisley shawl,
The table with the marble top, her quilts.
I went to see her just before snow came.
She said, 'I think I'll not be here for long,
And there is something you can do for me.
Find good homes for my plants, give them away
To folks who'll love them and will understand.
Unless someone can love them they will die.
The lemon tree that I grew from a seed,
The pink begonia, —we've been friends so long,
I know I'll worry till they find a home.'

"The row of plants along the table edge
Were all the same kind, white geraniums.
'My white geraniums *must* blossom,' she said.
'The snow is deep in winter. Sometimes
There isn't a road, only a snowshoe track
That freezes so hard you can walk on it
And not sink into the snow. Sometimes
A boy and girl want to get married
In winter and the girl can wear a wreath
Of my white geraniums. And sometimes up here

A baby doesn't stay with its folks too long
And I plant a posy with my white geraniums.'

"Well, now she's gone, and you can have your pick.
I noticed something queer when I was there
To take some callas home the other day.
I must have been beside myself to think
I felt her fingers laid upon my hand
When I took up her white geraniums."

O. D. Putnam

The first Jerome and Suzannah Hewitt House near Crane Mountain, Town of Johnsburg, Warren County, New York.

The Adirondack settlers who chose to remain in the mountain's harsh environment knew that they had to deal with nature's relentless force. Men and women worked as partners to provide the basic necessities of life for themselves and their children. With many men away for months at a time during the winter lumbering season, women had to rely on their own strength and common sense to maintain the home and to handle accidents, illness, or death. Neighbors or towns were often miles away; snow and cold prevented travel and communication. Women developed a strength of character as they faced the hardships of the environment and the isolation that nature brought. Their contributions to the family's survival placed them on a much more equal footing with men than many of their Victorian counterparts enjoyed.

Old Suzanne

"It's dreadful," Rachel said. "You've heard about her,
That woman living on the Spruce Hill Road,
Disgracing decent people who fear God
And live good upright lives; I shall complain
To our minister and he will see the town
Deals with her; she's a loose woman, I've heard
About her goings-on."

                 Her voice broke off.
Old Suzanne stood there in the gully path.
Her feet were hidden by October leaves
Blown into runnels of scarlet, her head
Covered with a brown shawl pinned tightly
Under her chin rounding her wizened face.
When she spoke fine wrinkles twisted her mouth
As if she struggled for words; then they came—
Taking their own way like spring freshet:

"Now, Rachel," the sounds cracked in her throat,
"You don't want to be too hard on that woman.
She don't care too much for new store fixings;
She's just fighting off going to the Poor Farm.
I know her; she's almost starving. . . . Rachel,
You don't know what it's like to be dog-gone poor.
There's only dirt for a floor in her house;
She has to put down straw for the winter.
And her man was just a good-for-nothing
Who ran off leaving her and the children
Without potatoes or even cornmeal.

"Rachel, I wouldn't tell the minister.
You don't know what you would do in her place.
There's something about 'throwing the first stone'
In the Book . . . you remember what it says."
The wind blew the red leaves down the gully;
Old Suzanne's eyes were fixed on something
A long way off; she didn't move or look
When Rachel turned and went back up the path.

The Last Tarring and Feathering

They had ways of keeping law and order
Long ago up here in the wilderness.
Sometimes one man alone in the township
Took it on himself to deal with sinners.
That was the way with our old Deacon Bowes.
He figured that the best way to keep order
Was to ride lawbreakers out of the town
After they'd been caught, and tarred and feathered.
The Deacon kept the tar ready to warm up,
And his friends were always saving feathers.

The Deacon was the neighborhood leader,
Right in his pew every Sunday, faithful,
Giving good advice to all the young folks.
He was a fine figure of a man, tall,
With longish hair swept back from his forehead
And a Roman nose. Strangers who saw him
Thought he looked just like George Washington.

Folks had heard for a long time about goings-on
At the old Hoadly place with Sal Pheemy
And a strange man who had come to live with her,
And how they were living there out of wedlock,
And they spoke to the Deacon about it,
Figuring on a tarring and feathering.
But he didn't seem to have the old vim
And kept putting it off, week going on week,
Until finally he was laid away
And nothing had been done about old Sal.

All her folks were gone, and she lived alone
On the farm; she'd come back to live there
After being away going on years—
Where, nobody knew. Now a man lived there.
They never went to church or neighbors.
Folks saw him with her helping in the fields,
And through the window when the lamps were lit.
And the folks that tried to live decent and godly
Planned to do a tarring and feathering.

The Deacon had a spot in Cedar Hollow
For such goings-on, and we picked up Sal
And the man one day and fetched them down
In a lumber wagon. The tar kettle
Was setting there filled with the Deacon's tar,
And we had brought sacks of chicken feathers.

When we untied them Sal stood up and screamed,
"Don't you dare touch my boy, I'm the sinner."
And the man stepped in front of her and shouted,
"Take me, I'm a man, I can stand tarring,
But don't you touch my ma; she ain't well now.
I wouldn't have come here only I was sick."
"They're lying," one of the boys said. "His ma.
Sal never got married; who was his pa?"
"Yes, if you're Sal's boy, who was your pa?"
The man tore off his close cap; his hair
Swung away from his forehead. "Look at me.
I'm the 'spit and image' of him, my ma says.
Look at me and you'll know who was my pa."

We looked; here was a younger Deacon Bowes—
The high forehead, the Roman nose, the features.
We remembered then how the old Deacon
Always *put off* tarring and feathering them.
And we thought of the young girl's leaving home
Years ago, sudden like, going away . . .
And never coming back or sending word.
And the thought came that it might be every man
Sometime comes to judgment. We took them
To their home and left them on the doorstep.

That was the last tarring and feathering
Up here in the wilderness, in our town.

Day Lilies

Come in, come in—the sitting room's right here.
We eat in here now; you'll find it warm and cozy.
Marcia'll set something on the table soon.
She's stewed pieplant and made some riz biscuits,
And there's a blackberry sauce and pork and greens.
I like to have folks enjoy their dinner,
The few that come—the old stage don't bring many.
They take the other road in their autos.
Times have changed; this used to be a toll road,
And I had three hired girls working for me
To get the dinners ready for city folks
Who came through on the old four-horse covered coach.
All that's left now is that rickety buckboard
That carries the mail and some wandering person
Who comes in here by chance or remembers
How the mountains looked from our windows.
There's Crane now with the notch and the low cloud
Always hanging below the tip peak.
They make me think of wool on carding combs.
And out to the west you'll see Gore Mountain,
A sprawling sort of mountain, running every way.
The state surveyor says Gore is the highest we have
In the county, but you'd never like it though
As well as Crane.

        You don't think I look well.
No, I'm not sick; I'm just kind of worn out.
Since Job's gone I have all the chores to do.
I'm not sick grieving; of course I'm lonely
For Job, but he's happy somewhere tinkering
With something he's found; men are that way.
Besides, I didn't ever know Job very well,
Although we lived together sixty years.
You don't always get to know a man well
Just because you happen to be married to him.
Besides, he wasn't one to care about things
That women like. Job loved our children
Like a man, but that isn't being a woman
And feeling their heart-beats day on day, waiting.
I never got very much comfort out of Job;
I'm wanting the baby I had last summer
That died. . . . I'm not touched; 'twas my baby
As much as the law could make it mine.
For I had baby fever even at my age,
And nothing would stop it till I got a baby.

You have baby fever when you're young sometimes,
But it's worse when your children are grown

And your grandchildren off in the world somewhere,
And your arms are empty when it comes spring.
And you see things growing, pineys and lilies
Pushing up in the garden, and you want to grow
With everything or make things as God does;
And you wake up longing in the spring nights
With the smell of crabapple blossoms
Coming through the window, choking up your throat;
And water tastes like fire.

                             I hitched up last year then
And drove down to the County House to see
If they had a baby left there for the taking:
There's plenty of babies at the County House
Most years that folks don't want. I got a baby,
A little girl. I tell you, I was happy.
I hadn't forgotten how to tend a baby,
And Job saved Jersey milk for it.
I think he liked it though he always scowled
When I was tending it. He thought about
The neighbors' talk, but I sewed baby clothes.
My grandchildren had taken all I had.
She lived only a year, and folks blamed me
For taking her; they said it wasn't right
For an old woman to bring up a child.
But I did everything a mother could.
The baby never cried, not from the first—
And babies that are going to live must cry.
One day I had her out by the flowerbeds
On a Thistle-Blow quilt laid on the ground.
I looked up from transplanting my day lilies.
She wasn't breathing. I picked her up
And ran to the house; I remember
Thinking all in a minute of my own babies
And everything they did, and smelling
That strong sickish sweet of day lilies,
For a stalk I had cut was hanging in my hand.

I'm old, but somewhere in this old body
And down in my heart I'm not old—I never can be.
I'm waiting to be called, and I know God will let me
Stay somewhere inside of the pearly gates long enough
To bring up that baby. I'm in a hurry
For fear she'll get so big she won't need me.

Marcia, this lady is waiting for her dinner.
While you're eating I'll run and pick you
Some of my day lilies.

Poverty Grass

Silver white on the hillsides,
Leveled by winds that pass
When summer is ripe with glory,
Shines the silver "poverty grass."

Tangled with brake and "moonshine"
(The everlasting flower)
It covers the barren hillsides
Where the tall green spruces tower.

It springs with April's tricklings
On the rocks that lie below;
It dies in the heat of summer
Before autumn winds can blow.

All through the sultry August,
Silver color in the sun,
The slender spears stand like pale shades
Foreboding frost to come.

When winter's blasts sweep downward
From off the mountain height
And bare the ragged places
Upspringing overnight,

We see the silver radiance,
This dead cold shining grass;
Between the drifts it gathers
Snow crystals as they pass.

And when the thaws are halted
By nights of freezing cold,
Each spear is bent, a bugle
Of ice with heart of gold.

Where this grass grows, there is no soil
To feed the roots of grain;
The cattle shun the silver slopes;
They know their search is vain.

Yet a forlorn wild beauty
Compensates those who see
These upland slopes when roaming
Old paths of memory.

O. D. Putnam

"Major General Hancock," the first train of the Adirondack Railroad, at the North Creek railway station.

In 1863 Dr. Thomas C. Durant began plans to build a railroad diagonally across the Adirondack Mountains. The only part of the plan that materialized was the Adirondack Railroad with a sixty-mile line, completed in 1871, from Saratoga to North Creek, a community on the Hudson River close to Johnsburg. Besides providing another means to transport lumber to the markets downstate, the railroad brought more visitors to the mountains. The stage would pick up passengers at the North Creek station and then travel to Indian Lake and on to Blue Mountain Lake, one of the most fashionable resort areas in the northeast. In 1889, after a stormy financial history, the Adirondack Railway Company was sold to the Delaware and Hudson Canal Company.[83]

The Jacob Davis House, North River, Town of Johnsburg, Warren County, New York.

From ten to eleven I spent most of the time at the home of Jacob Davis at North River. My mother's cousin, Frances Fuller, daughter of Duane Fuller, Blue Mountain Lake, married Jacob. Another daughter, Louisa Fuller, also lived at North River. She had married Nathan Davis; Louisa was then widowed.

Every two weeks I went through to Blue Mountain Lake with Jacob driving and tended the horses as he peddled yarn, pork, beef, buff mittens, socks, anything and everything. It was on one of these trips I got to know "Old Salt" and the Byrds. Also at "The Blue" I spent some time with Duane Fuller, boat builder, guide, game protector, my maternal grandfather's half-brother. (In later years Harry Armstrong allowed me to drive the Concord stage and the four horses from Indian Lake to "The Blue" one time.) At North River I taught myself to read music and came home able to play hymns. Then my father found an old melodeon for me.[84] [Photograph from an old postcard]

William Newell[85]

Forgotten except by one grandchild,
You sleep by the North River.
You knew the river well, driving logs each spring,
Living a shantyman's life by its headwaters.
There was no boat, and so you tried to cross
On a raft with two other men that day
In high water.

              Whether you slipped and fell
Or were pushed in because of a quarrel
No one knew; but you clung to a rock
In mid-river until you could hold no longer.
Then you waved goodbye to Lucinda
And your four little girls watching on the bank,
And the river swept you down into the gorge.

It was more than a hundred years ago,
But to me it is yesterday.
They found you and laid you there
Beside the North River that took your life
And set a white-birch tree
For a marker to grow up beside you.

I am the seed of the smallest daughter,
And through her I loved and remembered.
I came back to the river; old men showed me
The white-birch that guarded your dust.
I walk the earth with your heart in my breast,
With your blood in my veins, and I know
What no other knows—you forgave the North River
Even at the last when you rode its white water.

Balm of Gilead

It's curious how one can miss a tree
Down through the years. I've had so many friends
In the North Woods besides the human kind.
When I was small there weren't too many folks
Back where we lived—so I made friends with trees.
I loved white pine and a old yellow birch,
Grandfather of all birches; the gales took it down,
And when it fell my tears dropped on the bark.
But one tree somehow crept into my blood—
A kind of saint of trees—the Balm of Gilead.
We lumberjacks were careful trimming brush
Never to cut a Balm of Gilead tree.

We picked its buds in spring and made a salve.
Around each bud there is a ring of brown
Where the sap thickens on the outer sheath.
We gathered this for it had healing power.
We'd hardly go out on the lumber jobs
Without the healing ointment that it made;
We could heal every wound and hurt we knew
When we used Balm of Gilead for a cure.

The shanty men and lumbering days are gone;
There's no more first growth now, and second growth
Has been cut down and fire has done its work.
There's nothing left but memories and ghosts
And rotting logs to show where shanties stood.
But if you know where an old log road ran—
And follow on—you'll always find one friend
That the jacks knew, a Balm of Gilead tree.

Jim Kenyon's Horse

Sometimes animals mean more than humans.
I remember Jim Kenyon's old white horse
More than I remember him. The old horse
Used to stand up on his hind feet in Jim's orchard
Of wild apple trees he never grafted
And knock down apples with his front feet
And bite what he could off the lowest branches.
He was lean and spavined, and speckled-white
As if his hide had been doused with black pepper.
And his only idea seemed to be
To find something to stick between his ribs.

Jim's providing never reached the old horse.
His children went to school in zero weather
In thin little cotton coats and pants—
No underwear; they were lucky to have bread,
Let alone butter. He found something to eat
For the children, but the horse picked for himself.
In the summer he cropped grass along the road—
Jim didn't have land for grass—but in winter
He starved. If Jim had been kind he'd have shot him
And put him out of his misery. Time and again
After frost came I'd pass Jim's shack
And the horse would be pawing down sour apples.
Jim's children thrived and grew up somehow;
They're scattered around the world. I don't think of them.
But now and then I remember that old white horse
And the look in his eyes that life didn't mean much.
I see him as he used to stand on his hind feet
Trying to get those frosty apples between his teeth,
And I wish again what I used to wish when I saw him:
That if there's a horse-heaven with still waters
And green meadows and oats ripe for eating,
I hope Jim Kenyon's old horse finds them.

The "Bound-Out" Boy

O Johnnie Byrd was a "bound-out" boy
With no friends kind and true.
He was bound-out to serve Old Salt
On the road that led to "The Blue."

Old Salt kept a tavern on the road,
And he was hard to please:
He kicked the bound-out boy around;
The boy had no rest or ease.

Old Salt lost a leg with a pirate crew
And ashore he had to be,
But his stony heart was always out
In a pirate sloop at sea.

Poor Johnnie heard his gory tales
Of merchantmen he sank,
And of the loot the pirates took,
And folks who "walked the plank."

Old Salt would boast of his pirate ship,
A windjammer, queen of the sea,
And curse the fate that left him
High and dry on a barren key.

"She'd pick ten knots and then thirteen
Till we sighted an island palm;
Four days the doldrums held us fast
In the sloth of a tropic calm.

"She snapped a gaff off Hatteras,
But we were an able crew;
We haled aloft and spliced it fast,
And she never once heaved-to.

"Beam winds pummeled her blistered sides.
But we made for a Cocos Isle
And buried our chest in the shifting sand
Where it could stay awhile."

One day in a driving winter storm
Old Salt gave Johnnie the sack,
Without a coat in the biting cold,
And told him not to come back.

It was Jacob Davis who came along
A-sledding up to "The Blue."
He picked up Johnnie the bound-out boy
And carried him on through.

He wrapped him in buffalo robes;
Duane Fuller took him in,
And kept the bound-out boy well fed
Till the ice broke up that spring.

Duane Fuller (1830–1903), a native of Blue Mountain Lake, Hamilton County, New York, who lived almost opposite the [present site of the] Adirondack Museum, was a guide, boat builder, and skilled diver.

At seventy, my great-uncle Duane out-dived other guides to bring up a body from deep water in Blue Mountain Lake. He shot the largest panther ever shot at "The Blue." He was coming home from Mud Pond one night when the panther trailed him. He shot it through the eye, aiming at the gleam in the darkness. The next day, with his son, he went back and brought the panther to his home. The skin was purchased by General Hiram Duryea, the starch millionaire, who had a cottage at Blue Mountain Lake; he had the panther mounted crouched on a large limb, which was placed in his living room. Uncle Duane was six feet tall, straight as an arrow in his old age, kind, loveable, skilled. He is the man in my ballad who kept Johnnie Byrd all winter when he was turned out to freeze by "Old Salt." [Photographer unknown.]

The Game Protector

"Well, how are things?" I asked when I went in
To see Hank Birch. He's Game Protector now—
Six feet of lightning if you break the law.
He left his work. "I'm glad you came along.
Sit down awhile if you can find a place
In this old shop. I'm building guide boats now.
Today I'm steaming cedar roots for ribs.
I think when men are gone who build these boats
Hunting and guiding won't be quite the same.
I wouldn't want to use another kind. They're light
And strong. Your neck yoke don't set hard
Making the carries. If you build them right
They balance like a hair spring in a watch.
I thought before deer-jackers picked me off
I'd build a few more boats."

                           "What jackers, Hank?"
"I wish I knew. And there are so many ways
To break the law, that's only one of them.
When I was scouting round "The Blue" one day
I found a turnip patch up in the woods;
Whoever sowed the seed knew deer would come
And he could shoot one when he wanted meat.
I have to catch a man with the hides or points
To saddle on a fine. It's not the city sports,
But folks right here who give me trouble,
Like those who shot Ched Robilee's white horse.
They saw some leaves or branches stirring round
And never looked to see what might be there.
Ched put the price on; I hear he was paid
For every hair in that old horse's tail.

"I had some luck when I caught George McGinn.
He fed two hounds and kept a-running deer.
But men up here who really rile my blood
Are 'jackers'; they're the meanest hunters yet,
Paddling at night around the water's edge,
And when a deer comes down to drink,
Flashing a jack light straight into his eyes,
And shooting while he's dazzled by the glare.
I heard some men were jacking out on Minnie Pond,
And I went over on the next dark night.

"I heard the boat, though it was coming still,
With paddles under water, and I waited there.
Until some deer came down. They flashed the jack.

I raised my light and warned them off the pond.
They fired and put a bullet through my hat.
By luck, it was two sizes big for me;
The bullet creased my head; I bled a bit
But I stayed there till daylight.

                      "Where they went
I couldn't see; nor where they hid the boat.
Today someone went past my boat shop here
And tossed a bundle out. I opened it.
There was a haunch of meat, fresh killed I'm sure,
And this scrawl here. I'll read you what it said.
'Just keep your nose off Minnie Pond for good
And you'll have venison every day this spring.'
I'm going there tonight—and every night
Until I get those jackers. That's my job.
If they aim lower down, why, there will be
Another Game Protector at 'The Blue.'"

Skating the Mail from the Raquette

When I was lumbering up along "The Blue,"
From where the shanty stood I saw the lake
And Eagle and Utowana just beyond.
"The Blue" is a cup of islands in the spring;
Their hands of green show up among the firs.
And in the fall the red and yellow shines
To say the sap is running to the roots.
In wintertime the islands stand in glass,
Or mostly do, for gales sweep the lake clean.
I know most lakes that lie in the North Woods,
And all of them have had a song for me,
But always "The Blue's" music tuned my heart.

When I think back to the old logging days,
One winter at "The Blue" comes to my mind.
The roads were blocked; it might be several days
Before the stage could dig through from North Creek,
Or bring mail and medicines from Raquette Lake.
The ice was glare, and three guides volunteered
To skate down to the Raquette for the mail.

It was an all-day trip; I watched the lake
And caught them as they broke into "The Blue,"
Their pack baskets full up with all the mail,
Bending to keep their balance—three as one—
Searing the ice with their long racing strokes.
Behind, the sunset flared an orange sky.
They seemed to fly. Once long ago I saw
Three eagles soaring high against the sun.
And so these guides winged skating in the mail.

The lumbering's gone; there's nothing left to me
Except remembering, and these young guides
Will always be a picture I shall see
Until the time comes when my feet must take
The "hay road" to a town I've never seen.

Village of Griffin, Hamilton County, New York, c. 1882.

When I was eleven I was parked at Griffin with my Uncle Erastus Griffin (1842–1911) who fought with the 7th New York Artillery, Civil War. Griffin was at its wildest. My cousin and I were not allowed out to the ice parties and dancing on the ice Saturday evenings, but we went. We would have been disciplined had my uncle and aunt, not at home, known we even had been there. Expert skaters, we had long blades, not girls' skates, and so we could speed. We borrowed boys' suits and slouch hats from the tavern keeper Ed Duane, and no one ever knew we were not male. The tannery, a double one, was running full-blast and the logs were streaming into the river from outlying shanties. My aunt was in Chestertown nursing my father whose illness lasted a year. Uncle Erastus came home weekends; the rest of the time my cousin, Lena, twelve, and I ran wild through the country. We lived in my uncle's log house, with one wood stove for heat. During these years I knew many Adirondack characters my family did not know.[86] [Photograph courtesy of Ouida Girard]

Griffin

Towns die the same as folks; we think we know
The reason—change creeps on—it may be true,
But some have roots that bring up a new growth,
While others go and hardly leave a trace.
I wonder what Steve Griffin would say now
If he could walk again where Griffin lived,
The town named after him, the lumber king,
Builder of tanneries, a pioneer.

If you drive up through Johnsburg on the road
That runs to Oregon and on to Wells,
You'll find where Griffin built his lumber town.
The river widens out, the timbered hills
Lift up that once were climbed by shanty roads.
No one lived there when I went back last year
Except someone a-selling gas and pop.

When Griffin lived it was a roaring hive
On Saturday nights when all the jacks came down
From lumber shanties; no town in the west
Could cut a slice of life as wild for you.
There was square dancing on the Sacandog.
Men cleared the snow and rolled down the oil barrels
From the twin tanneries to build a fire
The fiddlers jigged old tunes till their strings broke
And spinning skaters circled round and round.

A footbridge crossed the river in those days
Just two boards wide; we footed over it
Like deer, in summer to the general store
Where the jacks did their trading come pay day.
Sometimes we called at the big boarding house.
There was a waitress lovely as a fawn
And shy as one, who served the pork and beans.
She looked like china when the light shines through.
A rich man stopped for dinner there one day,
He married her and took her far away.

You can see where the houses perched along the hills;
Counting the log and frame, perhaps two score,
But everything has crumbled and no one
Remembers the old names, except some jack.
Towns die the same as folks, and Griffin died.
The lumbering days are gone, the tanneries
Have rotted, and young trees and brush
Grow on the ridges where the houses gleamed
Their light: only a few remember where
Old Griffin stood beside the Sacandog.

As time went on I took three counties over,
Essex and Warren and wild Hamilton,
And sealed them in a book.

When Jeanne Robert Foster returned to live with her family in Chestertown in 1892 she continued her education, which had always been encouraged by both her mother and the Putnams. Her mother, Lizzy Putnam Oliver (later to be called Lucia N. Oliviere), graduated from Albany Normal School and taught in the Chestertown School. By the time Jeanne was sixteen she was teaching in country schools and boarding with families in the district. She would return home on weekends to help her father in the forest. She contributed most of her income to her family, a practice that continued until her parents died.

Her prose tells of shanty life, a life that would disappear in her time; her poems captured some of the lumberjacks' rhythms and ballads before they, too, were lost.

School No. 11, Mill Creek Road (Garnet Lake Road), Town of Johnsburg, Warren County, New York.

I realize my entire life has been conditioned by my early life in the Adirondacks. I lived on a remote farm in Essex County, in full view of Whiteface Mountain until I was sixteen. The next two years, I taught in red school houses in different parts of Warren County. My father knew many Adirondack ballads and loved to hunt out their sources. We buggy-drove in the three counties to hear other singers, and during these drives my father told me stories of the famous mountain characters he had known. When I was sixteen, I taught school near my father's last lumber job. I drove a skidding horse on the job, often fastening my own chains.[87]

The Old Minister

The school teacher went to spend one night
With each family in her district.
One day she told me a story. She had heard
Things were sparse with the old folks;
So she ate her dinner before she walked
To the place to spend the night with them.
In the morning the minister rose early
To make tea and toast for early breakfast.
When he put a plate on the old table
He set half a boiled egg beside the toast.
"Teacher," he said, "I hope you don't mind
Having only half an egg for breakfast.
We've only one hen; she does lay an egg
Most every day; my wife is so weakly
I give her that egg to keep up her strength.
I knew you wouldn't mind, schoolteacher,
If I gave you only half of the egg."
"Of course I told him that I never ate
Eggs for my breakfast, and he carried in
A whole egg to his wife. He prayed with me
Before I left; I don't forget that prayer."

Albro Tripp's Story
(from notes related by Albro Tripp)

In the month of October, in the year 1876, at the age of thirteen, I started on foot and alone for the northern part of Essex County, a distance of seventy-odd miles. The last of my journey was through the wilderness, and for a distance of about twenty-five miles there was not a clearing of any kind. There were bears and panthers, wolves, and lynx roaming through the woods, but I went along looking at the big trees, whistling, and hoping I would see a bear or a panther; also I was wondering if I was going to find work up there in the big woods as a lumberjack, for doing the work of a lumberjack was a he-man's job. I had never heard of a boy only thirteen working in a lumber camp. Well, after two days I came to a large lumber camp where about fifty men were employed. The man who was doing the lumber job was Sylvester Ross, and I wish to say right here he was one of the best men I ever knew. Religious, no. He was just a bighearted, understanding, honest man.

The men soon began to arrive and they were a husky lot. Some of them hadn't had a shave or haircut for two months or more. When the men were ready for supper Mr. Ross said, "Boys, here is a *man* I have just hired to drive the oxen. I want you to remember that he isn't as old as you are, and I want you to help him any way you can and be good to him." I said, "Please, Mr. Ross, don't say any more. I can fight my own battles. If any man commences on me for a fight he will wish he hadn't. They will soon find out I can take care of myself." How those men did laugh and yell! One big brawny Frenchman who would weigh over two hundred pounds hollered out, "I am betting three to one on the bullwhacker!" I worked with those men until the job was done, and never a man gave me a cross word, although I played plenty of tricks on them.

Few men know lumberjacks better than I do. I commenced to live with them when I was only thirteen years old, and I worked with them at least half of the time for the next twenty-five years. A lumberjack is strong, husky, and as rough as they make 'em. Ninety-nine percent of them will swear and curse, and nearly as many will get roaring drunk. A lot of them like a good fist fight, and all of them would help the man they fought with and licked if he wanted help. But a lumberjack is honest and hard working and always trying to earn his wages. I worked with many men in those years, but I never knew but one who was a thief. They are big-hearted, free with their money. In talking with you, one might call you a damn liar or a damn son-of-a-bitch, but those are just pet names if he is *smiling* when he says them.

They weren't churchgoers, but when anyone was down and out they would cheerfully give all they had to help, and if any thanks were offered they would probably tell the one they helped to go to hell. These were the old-time lumberjacks I knew, and yet down deep in my heart I am still one; and I would go farther to shake hands with one than with any other man I know of. We have nearly all passed away—the old-time lumberjack—and soon we shall all be gone. Why? Because there isn't any good enough timber left to make such men. If the Lord should shut His eyes to my many faults and let me walk through the Pearly Gates, I'll be disappointed if I don't find as large a percentage of lumberjacks there as men who were more churchly. But I wouldn't be surprised if one of them walked up to me and said, "How the hell did you get in?"

I will tell you something about my life as a bullwhacker when I was thirteen. I had to get up at about 4:30 in the morning and go to the barn and feed the oxen hay

124

and grain, clean out the stable, clean off the oxen with a card and brush, tie up a bundle of hay, and put some grain in a bag. I had to carry hay and grain into the woods for the oxen's dinner, for sometimes our work was two miles from the shanty. I would fasten the bag of grain on the oxen's horns, but the hay, which was tied up tight in a bundle, I had to carry. In the fall of the year I had to skid logs, as it was called.

I would fasten one end of a long chain to a ring in the ox yoke. The ring was in the middle of the yoke between the oxen. Then I was ready to go after the logs to haul to the skidway. The logs were scattered all through the woods where the choppers had chopped them down. Two men would make roads to the logs so that I could drive the oxen to them. I would haul from one hundred to two hundred logs a day to the skidway, where a man would roll them up into large piles. These logs were all cut thirteen feet long. Sometimes I had to haul these logs twenty to thirty rods, and sometimes I could haul two or three at one time if they were small, but only one if it was a large log. Sometimes the head end of the log would hit a big stone or a root, and then I would have to do some hard work to get it loose. So you see that to haul two hundred logs in one day to a skidway was quite a day's work for a boy of thirteen—for a man too. You would have to take a good many steps a day and say "Haw" and "Gee" and "Buck" and "Bright" a good many times a day.

About December first the snow was two feet deep and skidding logs was stopped. Mr. Ross went out into civilization to hire men who owned horses to draw logs for him. Mr. Ross had, I think, about eighty thousand logs on the skids, to haul to the river, a distance of about four and one half miles. My job now was to break out the roads and have them ready for the horse teams. Let's see what I had to do. In the morning I would hitch my oxen, Buck and Bright, onto a sled with hay and grain and my dinner on it. I usually started about 5:30 a.m. I had about four and one half miles to get to the woods where the logs were.

About the first of May bark peeling would commence, and then I would go into the woods to help peel bark. No, working in the woods hadn't made me into a dwarf, for the day I was sixteen I stood six feet tall and weighed 182 pounds. I could bend over backward, put my head on the floor, and rise back up again. I wasn't afraid to rassle any man who walked the northern Adirondacks with the exception of *one* man. I never believed in fighting if you could get out of it in an honorable way, but if one had to fight—yes, I had to sometimes—I remembered what father told me: Use your head to think with and your fists to fight with, and fight to win.

You might be interested in knowing that we peeled the bark from the hemlock trees before the trees were cut into 13-foot lengths. Bark peeling usually commenced about the first of May and would last about six weeks. The bark was used for tanning leather. Sometimes a jobber with twenty-five or more men peeling bark would divide them up into what were called crews, four men to a crew. One man chopped the trees down. One man trimmed the trees. One man cut through the bark clear around the tree every four feet, and then he slit or split the bark on top of the tree. Then the spudder, as he is called, peeled the bark. He did it with a tool called a spud, and it is shaped something like a chisel, only larger, weighing six or seven pounds. It has a handle about eighteen or twenty inches long. The sharp end of the spud was stuck into the slit on top of the tree and then worked down between the bark and the wood; and then with a quick pull of the spud toward the spudder, the bark was peeled from the side of the tree next to him. Then the same operation was used on the other side of the tree.

The spring I was sixteen I was working in the barkwoods for Mr. Ross. As I

Using oxen to haul cut logs out of the woods to where they could be transported to market.

By the mid-1800s demand for wood in the Northeast pushed loggers into the eastern and central regions of the dense Adirondacks. By 1850 New York led the country in lumber production with over seven thousand sawmills in the state, over two thousand of them in the Adirondacks. There were more than one thousand tanneries in the state; more than 250 of them were in the Adirondacks. Concern for the destruction of the Adirondack forests began to be voiced during the late 1860s primarily in the writings of Verplanck Colvin. He advocated the creation of an Adirondack Park and the preservation of the watershed mountains. By the early 1870s the New York State legislature began to respond to public pressure and created the Commission of Parks. The commission's report of 1873 recommended that the Adirondack forests be managed by professional foresters. This began the movement to preserve the Adirondack mountains. Photograph courtesy of the Adirondack Museum, used with permission of Macmillan Co.

remember it there were twenty men, five crews, four men to a crew. Each crew had to keep count of the trees peeled during the day. There was always more or less racing to see which crew peeled the most trees. From sixty to one hundred trees was a good day's work. There was one crew that was supposed to be the best crew in the woods. They were big, husky men, and the man who dropped the trees down was a man by the name of Ed Coward, a great chopper. There was no other crew expected to be able to peel as many trees as his crew could. But—they overlooked the Hayes crew.

The crew I was in was made up of all Hayeses. Ed Hayes chopped down the trees; he was a cousin of mine. I chopped the limbs off the trees. And next to me was my cousin Eugene Hayes who fixed the bark for the spudder. My brother Charlie spudded the bark. They were all good men; but with a boy of sixteen along to do the trimming, which was a man's job, we weren't supposed to have a ghost of a show. Mr. Ross would come around three or four times a week and count the trees to see if the right count had been given the night before; so every crew was careful to give the right count. When the bark peeling was over in about six weeks, Mr. Ross reckoned up the number of trees each crew had peeled, and to the surprise of all the men it was found that the Hayes crew had peeled thirty more trees than the Ed Coward crew. Whoops! Didn't the Hayes crew do some yelling! Mr. Ross gave us all five dollars apiece, and he placed his hand on my shoulder and said, "Truman, you are a boy in years, but you surely did a big man's work."

I will tell you a little about peeling bark. We usually commenced work about 6:30 in the morning and got through about 6:00 at night. We usually carried our dinner, and it consisted of bread, meat, beans and molasses, and sometimes cookies or fried cakes. Never butter. The plague of bark peelers is flies: big flies, little flies, and all kinds of flies except peaceful and gentle flies. There were the mosquitoes constantly yelling "coming, coming,"—and they were, by the thousands and millions, and each one trying to stick his bill into you first, and deepest. And then there were the billions of black flies that never told you they were coming but commenced work at once. They would crawl into your eyes, ears, nose, and mouth; in fact, any opening they could find. And then there was another small fly, so tiny you could hardly see him. We called him "all jaws." After a few billion had bitten you, your flesh would smart as if it had been burned. No, we didn't have anything to put on our faces to keep them away as we do now.

About noon we were ready for dinner. We uncovered our dinner pails, and sometimes a few hundred ants as well. They were always ahead of us, but these we could drive off, and they were the least of our troubles. But the flies never were so happy or mean as they were when we were trying to eat our dinner. They would light on our heads, and on our meat, by the hundreds. They got stuck in the molasses after we had put it on the bread. We just didn't have time to drive them away; so many a fly met an untimely death. The day's work done, we went back to the shanty and after supper went outdoors trying to get some rest, and the fly fighting started all over again. The boys would build three or four small fires out of wet, rotten wood, to make plenty of smoke. In that way we could beat those flies, but don't think they gave up. When 9:00 came and we were ready for bed, we found the flies still up and ready for business. We were ready for bed, but the flies weren't. So, we built smudges in the chambers to kill or drive out the insects, and the room would be so blue with smoke it would kill nearly anything. There was a small window in each end of the room; so the smoke got out finally. and after a while we went to sleep, and then nothing short of a panther could have awakened us.

O. D. Putnam

Fred and Charlie Bates peeling bark.[88]

Folk tales and shanty songs created a mystique about the lumberjacks who worked the Adirondack forests. Many of the men fit the image of the coarse, hard-working and hard-drinking drifter with unbelievable strength. But the ballads often failed to mention that the lumbercamps, offering pay that was comparable to that in the cities, provided a means for many men to earn enough money to buy land and support a family. Many French Canadians and Irish families settled in the Adirondacks for this reason.

Lumberjack

The breed is gone, the old-time lumberjacks.
They were big-hearted, free with what they earned;
Honest, hard-working, rough-and-tumble men;
And if they cursed, that didn't mean a thing.
Some of them liked to get a stomach full
On Saturday night if they went into town,
And some would fight if you just looked at them
And didn't smile, but grudges weren't kept.
And they'd go a long space to help a jack.

One winter when I worked at Newcomb Lake
And Charley Bates was straw boss on the job,
We hired a Frenchy down from Canada.
We'd lost a chopper and we needed him.
He didn't speak a word of English talk,
But he could chop; two skidding horses might,
If they were fast, keep up with what he cut
Down in one day. One time he lodged a tree
And when the second fell it broke his leg.

Now it was winter and the snow was deep,
And it was forty miles down to the Creek.
We put a wagon box on top of sleigh
Filled up with straw and hitched up the horse,
And I drove out to get him on a train.
With the deep snow and shoveling out the drifts
It took two days for me to land him where
A doc could fix his leg and see he went
Back to Saint Marie where he lived.

We had an Indian greaser at the camp
Who spoke a little French, and he found out
That Frenchy had a wife up in the north,
And children—there were six of them, we heard.
So when he left the camp the jacks shelled out,
And he left with enough to see him well.

O. D. Putnam

Shanty picture, probably taken near Johnsburg.

My unsung father with his shanty life, his devotion to trees, his deep emotions, love for friends, largely shaped my mind, my life. We were constant companions as long as he lived. We understood the people in the back districts of the mountains.[89]

Shanty Days

It's hard to find the log roads in the woods
Or where they were; the shanty days are gone,
But still I think the old days in the woods
Will be alive as long as one remembers them.
Sometimes it's hard for me to figure out
Why no one talks about old shanty days
Except myself in these parts hereabout.

Maybe I've lived too long. . . . All men know now
When lumber's needed there's a power sawmill
They set up in a stand of spruce and pine.
There's hardly men alive who slept on bunks
In lumber shanties deep in the North Woods,
Choppers and limbers and the men who hauled the logs
Down to the river for the "run" in spring,
Or know a skidway, or how many "markets" cut,
Or why we peeled the hemlock bark in May.
If you speak up they only stare at you
And wonder where you've slept the years away.

My heart aches—for the lumbering days are gone
Though you may still find cuts in the deep woods,
If you remember where to look for them,
That led to big forgotten lumber jobs
With log shanties that bunked the men.

It was a clean hard life. Men went in when snow came
And didn't take the hay-road till the spring.
There were some farmers too who hired out
With regular lumberjacks when crops had failed
To earn a little cash to help the farm.
It was a great adventure when a boy
Went into the lumber-woods for the first time.
He had to earn his grub, to fight his way
Till the jacks saw he had the stuff it took
To hold his own and keep big bullies in their place.

We used to box and wrestle in the woods;
We stuffed our sheepskin leggings on our hands
For gloves and squared off in the long bunkhouse
After the grub. When I was sparring with Bob Smith
The men held up a broomstick just between
Our waists to teach us to stand up and box.
Bob swung too low, I biffed him on the nose.
I backed away and stumbled and went down
Upon a pile of wood beside the stove;
He came on fast and fell atop of me;

I was so young and scared I grabbed his waist
And hung on so he couldn't lift a mitt,
And then we laughed. We both were young and green,
And the old jacks dared us to fight again.

It was a good clean life—the crash of falling trees,
The smell of balsam and of spruce and pine,
The chittering of the jays, the skidways piled
With sappy logs, the resin on our hands,
The cook house with its pans of pork and beans
And johnny cake. . . . We had enough to eat.

The shanties—years have rotted them away,
Although you still can see where one has been
And what was once a clearing, by the logs
Of the foundation of the big bunk house.
I find them when I tramp old shanty roads,
Or what is left of them, grown up with brush.
Sometimes I sit down on a mossy stump
And shut my eyes. . . . The shanty days come back,
I hear the choppers' axes on the trees,
The sound of limbing and the clank of chains
Hauling the logs down to the old skidway,
The shouts of "Timber!"—and I get the smell
Of slashed-down pine sweet with its resin sap.

It don't last long. I open up my eyes
And struggle back to what we call life now.

Skidding Logs with Billy

From my earliest years I had been familiar with shanties and shanty life. When I was sixteen, and after I had finished sixteen weeks of school teaching at the Spruce Mountain School, I went over into the last lumber job father took—since he was failing in health because of an accident—with my horse Billy.

Billy was a bay gelding, a small, wiry horse. I had bought him from a defunct livery stable at a low price because he was eleven years old. We lived at Chestertown in the old Braley house on which father had built a small barn. We had left the old Foster place because Mother and Father Foster had returned from long pastoral service on the circuits to occupy the house.

Since we had an old buggy, I bought Billy to commute between the Putnam farm and Chestertown. Billy knew the meadows and the interior of the old barn as well as any horse there might. As we raised oats on the Foster farm and cut hay there, we fed Billy well, and he soon developed a strong affection for me. In the summer I turned him out at times on the Tripp farm at Darrowville. I did not have to pay for this pasture, as I had boarded sixteen weeks with Andrew Tripp and had, he considered, helped him. He was a hunchback with a withered arm permanently attached by a skin-fold to his chest. He was only about four and one-half feet tall, but he had a fine intelligence and a rather handsome face.

Father's financial judgment had never been good; mother and I feared a loss on the Spruce Mountain job. The skidways were beside the Warrensburg-Chestertown Road, and the logs were skidded from the job that was beyond the old Thomson place off the Kelm Pond Road, which was then called the Spruce Mountain Road, left side going south. On the weekends we came back to Chestertown. On a Monday, father and I would start at 4:00 a.m. for the job, driving Billy hitched to an old cutter. The other horses were kept at Thomson's.

One cold morning, arriving just at daylight opposite the job, we saw father's head chopper, Powell Hill, lying on the crust, apparently dead, on his way to the job. Father thought he must be dead—frozen to death. But Powell was saturated with alcohol. He drank heavily. However, after we got him up and into the Thomson farmhouse and fed him a hot breakfast, he chopped all day. I have never, even knowing the Canadians, known a faster or more expert chopper than Powell Hill.

Well, Billy the ex-livery horse soon learned the tricks of his job: when to hold, when to leap aside, and so on, and when I could I helped father with Billy. No one else ever skidded with Billy; there were other horses. Sometimes I had to have help with the chains, but not with the drag down to the skidway. From the skidway the logs were drawn to Glens Falls.

1970

Log drive on the Hudson River.

Millions of huge logs floated into the Hudson River from other rivers and streams farther north. Once the lumberjacks moved the logs into the rivers, log drivers worked quickly to get them to mills in Glens Falls and Albany during the short period in the spring when the Hudson was high and fast. These men risked dismemberment or death for the higher wages they received as drivers. They worked from before daylight until dark in cold water, often in freezing weather. A driver's skill and courage were tested when logs jammed. He had to move quickly to the obstructing log, chop it free, and move out of the way before the jammed logs broke loose. A mistake meant he could be crushed or drowned. Photograph courtesy of the Adirondack Museum.

Garron's Rock
(based on an old Adirondack ballad)

Come all my gay young Shanty Boys
Wherever you may be.
I hope you'll pay attention
And listen unto me,
Concerning six bold Shanty Boys
So manful and so brave.
It was at the jam at Garron's Rock
They met with a watery grave.

It was on one Sunday morning
As you are soon to hear,
The logs they were piled mountain high
And we could not keep them clear
Until our boss cried out. "My boys
With hearts avoid of fear,
We will break the jam on Garron's Rock
And for Eagantown we'll steer."

They had not rolled off many logs
When the boss to them did say—
"My boys, you'd better be on your guard
For the jam will soon give way."
No sooner had he spoke those words
When the jam did break and go.
It carried away those six brave lads
And their foreman, young Monroe.

When the rest of these bold Shanty Boys
These sad tidings came to hear,
In search of their dead comrades
To the river they did steer.
One of their headless bodies there
Did fill their hearts with woe.
All cut and mangled on the beach
Lay the head of young Monroe.

They took it from the water there
And they smoothed his drenched curls.
There was one fair form among them—
A fair Canadian girl;
There was one fair form among them,
A girl from Saginaw town,
Whose moans and groans would rend the skies,
For her true love was drowned.

Young Clara was a noble girl,
Likewise the raftsman's pride.
Her mother was a widow
Who lived by the riverside.
The wages of her own true love
The boss to her did pay,
Likewise a large subscription
From the Shanty Boys next day.

The Reckoning

We stepped from the shanty at sun-up
And over our heads was the glow
That touches the woods in the morning
When the treetops are spattered with snow.

Our moccasins creaked on the log road;
They scraped like an old violin
That's being tuned up for a shindig,
Or the scratch of hard resin on tin.

Old Pow had his ax on his shoulder,
Double-bitted and keen as a knife.
As a chopper he held that ax dearer
Than kinfolk or maybe his life.

The swampers had cleared up an acre.
Old Pow bit his ax in a tree;
When it fell it lodged in another
And Pow set his eloquence free.

He cursed till the jays stopped their chatter,
And the squirrels on the boughs sat stock still;
When he stopped to take breath for a minute,
He'd a new lot of black oaths to spill.

Then he struck his ax into a veteran
Smooth far up as eye could reach;
When Pow shouted "timber" it came down
Out of line-up and lodged in a beech.

Then Pow shook his fist at the sunrise
And shouted, "You've done it, by gee.
In a minute we'll have a reckoning.
Old Fellow, You'll answer to me."

"You've lodged both my trees—I'm a chopper.
If you're Boss, I'll say You're not fair.
That tricky young parson is lying
When he says that You're on the square."

"I'm a chopper. I know that You lodged them. . . ."
Just then from above came a sound,
The groan of big trees that were straining
Before they crashed down to the ground.

The big beech came down with the veteran
While Pow stood there having his say.
We yelled, but he just went on cursing
The One he thought planned it that way.

I jumped for his arm but I missed him.
I swung to the left like a flash
For the hemlock and big beech that second
Came down in a thundering crash.

Old Pow never knew what had struck him,
The hand of his God or a tree,
But we'd heard him shouting that morning:
"There's a reckoning between Him and me."

You may spill a loose tongue in the shanties,
But out where His trees touch the blue,
Don't curse Him, just take what He's sending
Or a reckoning's coming to you.

Men stacking hemlock bark to ship or draw to tanneries.

Of softwoods logged in the Adirondacks, white pine was sought for premium lumber logs, hemlock bark was used in the tanning of leather, and red spruce was used for paper pulp. Millions of hemlocks were cut, the bark stripped, stacked, and shipped to tanneries. The rest of the tree was left in the woods to return to the soil.

Lumbering reached its peak during the last part of the nineteenth century. Tanneries began to decline when chemicals replaced the tannin of the hemlock bark. Nearly 700,000 acres of land that had been stripped of its conifers and other forest growth had reverted to New York State for unpaid taxes. This and other land still held by the state in both the Adirondack and Catskill Mountains was the beginning of the New York State Forest Preserve, established by law in 1885, with such lands required to "be forever kept as wild forest lands." In the years immediately following, New York State's Forest Commission flagrantly abused this law. In 1892 the Adirondack Park was established; in 1894 the Forest Preserve was given stringent constitutional protection when the famous "forever wild" covenant was added to the New York State Constitution. Ultimate control for the use of Forest Preserve lands was placed in the hands of the citizens of New York when the constitution went into effect the following year.

Things That Do Not Change

I can look down here over the valley
And forget the fingers of Change
Working upon the cities out yonder.
I can forget everything that happened
From my birth. The things I do not forget
Are the things that happened before I came:
The green valley; and the tall elms spreading
Like parasols upon the beaver meadow;
The crawling line of the creek; the black alders;
The fringe of bushes that marks the wagon road;
The hills of my sheep pasture with sweet fern
And pennyroyal savoring the air when the dew falls
And the south wind chitters in the pines.

Beyond the pasture, the mountains lie
Talking to themselves and to the winds
Of the stars that shine over their summits
Or of some unseen ladder ascending
Like Jacob's from their peaks unto heaven.
Sitting here with my pipe in the chipyard
Beside the woodpile on a spring morning,
I forget everything; nothing has happened
To me ever since I was born. There was
A man like me who knew certain people
Who lived the life of men here among men.
Sometimes I see his life like an old road
Leading nowhere; and I think he was a curious man
To be wanting all the pain that he had
When he might have sat all his life in the chipyard
Looking out on the things that do not change:
In a twinkling, having a slow hazy thought
Of a place so steadfast that the gray mountains
Seem to have been created by a moment.

The Wilderness Is Strong

Here in the wilderness folks will tell you
To be careful about the place you live,
For there's something in the mountains
And the hills that is stronger than people,
And you will grow like the place where you live.
The hands of the mountains reach out
With bindings that hold the heart forever.

Those who live close to the high mountains
Are different from men along the rivers
And those on the intervales and cleared farms.
The mountain men know one another by signs,
And river men have their own kind of speech.
And strangest of all are the folks on islands
Who always hear the lapping of water
And see the tall scarlet cardinal flowers.
If an island man's children leave their home
They always return; they are drawn back.

Wilderness people are a special breed.
They have something that's not hearing or seeing
Reaching out from the mountains to touch them.

State Land

"Father, why did you make the timber lot
State land? If you must sell, why not to us?
Have you forgotten that your sons must live,
And timber's growing scarcer every day?
When the state took the mountainside we thought
That it would have no more. Now you have sold
Two hundred acres of fine timber land,
And we who follow you must go without
All that the land would bring in years to come,
With its rich stand of hemlock and of pine."

"I think, my sons, that you in time will see
My reasons; you are young and moving out
Upon the tide of what to me is strange.
You have new ways to struggle and to win,
More than I had, who cleared land for my farm.
I have watched spoilers come and take away
So much I hardly know my township here.
I gave the mountainside to keep it wild,
Free for the life that it has had so long.
The trail will always be what it is now.
The summit, with its scrubby balsam trees,
A playground for the deer and porcupine.
The timberland—well, I walked over it
Before I gave the deed to join its soil
To our wilderness. Beyond my line
I looked down on the havoc of the years,
Dude ranches sprawling where farmhouses stood.
I have no quarrel with what you call 'our times,'
But my heart spoke: I must preserve this land.
I walked over the land from end to end;
Looked at the garnet outcrop, and the ledge
Of quartz where we found native amethyst,
And from the serpentine we used to carve into inkwells.

"I listened to the brook. The yellow
Lady-slipper grows there, and the pink,
And other flowers that fly the feet of men.
I touched the trees; somehow they sing to me;
The pine and hemlock leaning to the wind;
The birdseye maple and, where sun could touch,
The slippery elm we used for medicine.
There is a deadfall up there in those woods
They say the Indians built long, long ago.
It's rotted down, but you can see the way
The Indian hunters planned to catch a bear.

As I walked on I prayed this land might be
A sanctuary of our wilderness
That keeps the human soul close to its God.

"There are still two hundred acres of cleared land,
The beaver meadows, and the sugar bush and orchards
For my sons. In future years you will come here
And touch the trees as I have done,
And think that I did right."

Crane Mountain, Warren County, New York

You [Paul Schaefer] have been where you have looked at Crane in all the special beauty it wears this season of the year. I envy you and picture it in memory as I have seen it many times. There is much to write, but first I want to tell you of my secret trysting spot with Crane.

If, when you go to the old Elliot Putnam place—"Francis Putnam place" as we once called it—you will walk toward the mountain directly from a point that would be about the exact location of the old Putnam house. You will cross the brook, of course, and keep on through the woods until you come to a stretch of the mountain where it rises *straight as a wall* from the terrain so that one may stand straight and lean against it. I found this stretch long, long ago and, in my young girlhood—up to the last summer I spent with Elliot—I would walk secretly and *lean* against the mountain, sometimes facing it and putting my hands out either side. There seemed to be a strong force passing through me, so untamed, wild and beautiful that there are no words for it. But I know this force remained with me, helped me manage my difficult life, sent me to "five seas" if not to the "seven," flowed as courage in my blood . . . and never left me—not *even today*.[90] [Photograph courtesy of Paul Schaefer]

Crane Mountain

(for Paul Schaefer)

How can I lift my mountain before your eyes,
Tear it out of my heart, my hands, my sinews,
Lift it before you—its trees, its rocks,
Its thrust heavenward;
The basic cliffs, the quartz of the outcrop,
The wide water in the cup of the lower summit,
The high peak lifting above the timberline
Gathering the mist of fifty lakes at sunrise;*
The waterfall tumbling a thousand feet,
White with foam, white with rock-flower in summer;
The wreathing of dark spruce and hemlock,
The blood splashes of mountain ash,
The long spur to the north golden with poplars;
A porcupine drinking, bending without fear
To his image?

When darkness shall be my home,
Eternal mountain, do not leave my heart;
Remain with me in my sleep,
In my dreams, in my resurrection.

*Original line: Gathering fifty lakes that look up at sunrise;

APPENDIX

MARTHE
A Play in One Act

by

Jeanne Robert Foster

Editor's Note: *In her Adirondack literary legacy Jeanne Robert Foster left two short plays. This one, based on her poem "Mis' Meagan" in* Neighbors of Yesterday, *was published in 1927 under the name of Noel Armstrong in* Fifty More Contemporary One-Act Plays *and was later produced in the Pasadena Theater in California. Although* Marthe *had been previously published it is included in this volume both because of its significance as a part of her contribution to Adirondack literature and as an example of Jeanne's versatility as a writer.*

Persons of the Play

MARTHE RIGNEY.............................. An aged Irishwoman

MARY DAVIS................................... Her elderly neighbor

FANNY WASHBURN.......................... Another elderly neighbor

DAVID LELAND............................. A peddler of eggs and butter

LUCIE OLIVER.............................. A young school teacher

JOHN DAVIS................................... A young man

The time: The year 1890
The action takes place in the afternoon and evening of one day.

The place: A farming community in the mountains of New York.

Scene: *The stage is a large square room with four windows, the kind of room that in an Eastern farmhouse is used for both living room and kitchen. The walls are wainscotted elbow-high with unpainted hard wood that has turned brown with age. Above the wainscotting, the walls are hung with a striped wall paper. The floor is of wide smooth boards scrubbed a glistening white. On the floor are faded braided and hooked rag rugs. At the back of the room on the right, is an open door that leads into a bedroom. This door is open and one sees a high four-poster bed covered with a blue and white woolen counterpane. At the back of the room on the left a door with upper panels of glass opens into a woodshed. On the left side of the room another door opens into a pantry. On the wall near the pantry door is a shelf of wood, unpainted and brown with age and the smoke of many fires. On the shelf are old blue china cups and saucers and plates, a sugar bowl, and a cheap clock and a kerosene lamp. In the middle of the room is an old-fashioned stove with a high oven and doors in front of the fire box that may be flung open to give the effect of a fire place. On the walls are two crayon portraits in hideous tawdry gilt frames: one is the likeness of a plain-featured young Irishwoman, the other is that of a handsome young Irish lad leaning on a stick. Both have apparently been copied from daguerreotypes. A tawdry bright colored calendar of the current year—1890—hangs over the table and a yellow almanac hangs under the clock shelf suspended from a peg by a loop of string.*
On the high oven of the stove are old-fashioned flat irons with bright patchwork covers on their handles. Behind the stove is a woodbox covered with the same striped paper that decorates the walls. Four unpainted wooden chairs are ranged stiffly against the three walls. A chair similar to those against the walls is on the right of the stove well out toward the middle of the room. Mary Davis sits

in this chair knitting. She is an old woman in her seventies, sprightly, modern-minded and energetic. She wears a shabby but decent black silk dress made with a basque and a full gathered skirt. She has a bit of old lawn pinned about her throat with an oval gold brooch. Her one bit of flair is a pair of antique earrings that match the brooch.

On the left of the stove but toward the side wall, Fanny Washburn is sitting. She is slightly younger than Mary Davis, a simple, kindly, credulous soul. Her dress is a faded wine colored cashmere made with a polonaise and a plain skirt with a flounce. She has yellowish mull ruches in her high straight collar and in the edges of her tight cuffs. She is gentle, subdued, and resigned in manner. Her hands are folded on her lap.

Near the stove on the left, ranged so that the three women make an arc of a circle, Marthe Rigney is sitting in a wide deep wooden arm chair cushioned in red calico. She is a hard-minded old woman. Her face is Irish, squarish, masculine and grim, her eyes bright. When she speaks her voice will have the note of time and her hard nature—a dry irritating rasp. She wears skirts of faded blue calico and a light lemon-colored basque. A large plain white cotton handkerchief is pinned around her throat fichu fashion. Her stockings are white and wrinkled around her ankles and her coarse leather pumps have been made by cutting off the tops of a pair of Congress gaiters. She wears a cap of fluted yellowish muslin with strings that dangle on either side of her face. Her hair is scanty but not white. It has been black and is a grizzled grey. She is smoking a blackened clay pipe which she fills from time to time from a pocket in her skirt. Near her chair on the left is a small semi-circular green plant stand. On the plant stand is a paper of smoking tobacco. (The women wear dresses ten years behind the styles of the period because fashions did not change in the remote mountain hamlet where they lived. Dresses were cherished possessions and lasted many years.)

MARTHE RIGNEY: And what do folks say about me, Fanny Washburn? Mary is always hinting that they have something to say.

FANNY WASHBURN: I'm not one to be carrying tales, Marthe. What does their talk matter? We all have to live our own lives. Your way aint their way.

MARTHE: But I want to know—what do they say?

MARY: I'll tell you what they say, Marthe. No use to ask Fanny. She's too chicken-hearted to tell you. They say . . . you're *hard as nails.*

MARTHE: Hard as nails. . . . [*She chuckles.*] I don't mind that. What else do they say?

MARY: Oh, a lot of things. They aint forgot how you drove off that handsome Michael Callahan that wanted to marry you when you was young and broke his heart, and they aint forgot you married your hired man—just in name—to keep him on the farm to do your work, and they aint forgot the hard bargains you've drove. . . .

FANNY: Mary . . . . we've always been friends, you and I and Marthe. Let's forget that old talk. Its nigh dead and buried. We're too old to be carrying scandal. Besides, you'll hurt Marthe's feelings.

MARTHE [*Motioning her to be silent*]: No, she wont hurt my feelings. According to most folks round here, I haven't got feeling. I don't remember having any myself. You're better off without 'em. I've lived just as I wanted to and I aint sorry. You tell folks they wont gain nothing talking about me. I've always had my own way and what folks said didn't matter.

FANNY [*Trying to change the subject*]: Let sleeping dogs lie—that's what I think. Marthe, why don't you have some house plants? You've got that nice stand to have them set on.

MARTHE: I never had no time for flowers. I don't know one kind from another. I had enough to do raising corn and rye and buckwheat without fussing with flowers. [*To Mary*] Where's that pesky butter and egg man, Dave Leland? Why don't he come fer my eggs? Go and look out the door and see if his wagon is up the road. [*Mary Davis goes to the window.*]

MARY: He's here. He's coming round to the woodshed door. [*Knocking*] [*Calls*] Come in . . . come in.

MARTHE: Go and get the eggs. [*Mary Davis goes into the pantry.*]

[*Dave Leland comes in through the woodshed door. He is a roughly dressed farmer with high boots and a soft felt hat.*]

DAVE: How de do, how de do, Miss Rigney. How de do, Mis' Washburn.

MARTHE: You're late, Dave.

DAVE: Yes, I've been up on Pride's Hill gathering up eggs and butter. The road's bad up there. I had to drive slow. One of my hosses is lame.

MARTHE [*To Dave*]: Dave, you've known me a long time, aint ye?

DAVE: Why yes, Mis' Rigney.

MARTHE: Do ye ever hear folks talking about me? [*Mary Davis comes out of the pantry with a basket of eggs. She stands holding the eggs.*]

DAVE: Talking about ye—what do ye mean, Mis' Rigney? I reckon the best of us gets talked about.

MARTHE: Do they say I'm a *hard* woman? Oh, ye needn't be touchy about telling me . . . tell me what they say?

DAVE: Well, seeing as you've asked it and no offense, they say ye aint no heart, Mis' Rigney.

MARTHE: Is that so? Well, you tell 'em its true I aint, and what's more, I don't want one either. I've lived my life and worked my farm myself and I'm not beholden to anybody. I'll live as I please and die as I please and its none of folk's business.

MARY [*To Marthe*]: Are you going to get through this nonsense and count these eggs? Put out yer pipe. I never saw such a woman as you are—smoking, smoking all the time. The house smells like a shanty from yer dirty old pipe. Put it on the hearth and count the eggs while I go and get the sticks. [*She goes to the woodshed to get the sticks.*]

MARTHE [*To Fanny*]: Ye never wanted to smoke, did ye, Fanny?

FANNY [*Scandalized*]: Me? No, I never did. Me! Asmoking before my children and grandchildren!

MARTHE: Well, I never had no children or grandchildren so I can smoke. [*Counts the eggs*] One, two, three, four, one, two, three, four, one, two, three, four, one dozen; one, two, three, four, one, two, three, four, one, two, three, four, two dozen; one, two, three, four, one, two, three, four, one, two, three, four, three dozen. [*To Dave*] You can have 'em for fifty-cents a dozen, Dave.

DAVE: I aint paying but forty-five, Mis' Rigney. Eggs has gone down.

MARTHE: Trying to rob a poor woman, aint ye. [*Mary Davis returns with the sticks.*]

MARTHE: Where's the knife?

MARY: Here is your knife. Now cut the notches for the eggs. Why didn't you ever learn to read and write?

MARTHE: One, two, three—three dozen to sell today. [*She runs her hand over the old notches.*] I tell ye, I've got the hens for laying eggs. [*Recollecting herself*] Why didn't I learn to read? Well, I learned to *count* if I didn't learn to read, and that's something you've never had much need of with your spendthrift ways. That's about all I had time to learn, Mary Davis. What do you know about working land and making a living— you, who have sons and daughters to keep you in silk?

DAVE: Well, well, I must be getting on with my load. Are you taking the forty-five for the eggs, Mis' Rigney?

MARTHE: I suppose I'll have to. Put the money in the blue tea cup on the shelf. Count it out to me first. [*He counts out the sum.*] Now, here they are. [*Hands the basket to him*] And see that ye put the basket back in the wood shed after ye empty it.

DAVE [*He takes the basket, counts the money in her hand, then puts it in the blue teacup on the shelf.*]: Goodbye, Mis' Rigney, goodbye, Mis' Davis, goodbye, Mis' Washburn. See you next week. [*Dave Leland goes.*]

FANNY [*Looking at the clock*]: Land, I must be getting home. [*She goes in the bedroom and puts on a wrap and a bonnet. She goes up to Marthe and gives her a pat on the shoulder.*] Don't you be caring what folks say. Goodbye, Mary. Come down to see me when you can. Goodbye, Marthe. [*She goes out the wood shed door.*]

MARY [*Sitting down in her chair*]: Well, you've found out what folks say about you. I could a told you any time fer forty years back.

MARTHE: Yes, I found out what kind of a neighborhood I live in. Folks that'll spend their time talking about a poor old woman with no children to stand up fer her or any kin this side the water.

MARY: Well, you might o' had some! Why didn't you marry when you were young and have a family to keep *you* in silk? I know *why* you didn't. You thought too much of your land and the money you'd saved. I remember you said once that you didn't know but children would be wasting what you had and anyway you couldn't tell how children might turn out. Always thinking of yourself when you might have been doing what other folks did and having what they had—always thinking of yourself and your land.

MARTHE: Why didn't I marry when I was young? Well, there was a gossoon running here and trying to be courting me when I was young. He was a well-favored lad, but he had nothing, *nothing,* I tell you, not even a cow, and I thought what a fool I'd be, making off from my pa and ma and the land, and trying my luck with a stranger. He was always singing a song, an Irish song, you wouldn't know it, *Pastheen Finn* is the name, and he was that tall y'd think a tree come walking down the road when y'd see him coming. You'd thought I was a queen to hear his tongue, Mary Davis. The things he said were like burning coals—I remember them yet. But I was young and hard and I sent him away. I never knew whether I wanted him or whether I didn't, but I knew I did want the land. And as fer thinking o' myself as you say, and the land . . . maybe I did. Who worked the land and got a living after my pa and ma were old? You never plowed all day with horses or oxen ugging through greensward with the plow catching on roots. Did you ever sow and reap and burn off fallow land and be out toiling from sunrise to dark? No, you never did and that's why you don't know what *land* means and why I liked to sit here when I had my eyes looking over the fields and thinking about nothing else; [*Smokes again*] and as for children—they're for soft women who can wear silk like you, Mary Davis. They mightn't o' been children I'd like . . . and I might a been leaving them alone after a few years. Put these sticks back in the shed.

[*Mary Davis trots out to the shed and hangs the sticks on their peg. She comes back with another armful of wood which she puts in a woodbox that stands at the back of the stove. She stands by the stove brushing the wood-dust from her apron. The stove is red with fire although it is a warm day in early autumn.*]

MARY: Land, but it's hot in here! You *do* feel the least bit of chill in the air. Shall I make tea and start supper now?

MARTHE: You can make some biscuits. There's flour and lard and milk in the pantry. And you can make some tea. Put it on and let it boil. I don't like tea unless it's boiled half an hour.

[*She empties her pipe by knocking it out on the hearth and lays it down. Then she walks with difficulty to the window and peers out. Mary Davis, who has gone into the pantry, comes back with a teapot in her hand. She pours water into the teapot from the tea kettle steaming on the stove and sits down again in the rocker.*]

MARY: I don't see how you keep your health drinking tea that's boiled and strong as lye. But you can stand more than most folks. You went on hounding that good-for-nothing hired man you married until I should have thought 'twould have worn you out!

MARTHE [*Groping back from the window*]: The good-fur-nothing I married to keep on the place! Well, the ceremony was all he had and that was more than he deserved. He gave me a bad time. He wouldn't stick to *his* bargain. 'Twas agreed that if I married him he would stay here and work the farm for sake o' having the land when—when I wouldn't want it any more. He was flighty and when I'd gone to town and married him, he was never satisfied and kept sulking round and wouldn't work and begun buying everything and having store debts charged to me. I was near ruined with the debts so I drove him off. I never heard from him but once.

MARY: That was when he fell off a load of logs and was killed, wasn't it?

MARTHE: Yes. He never knew anything after he fell and when they got him up here there wasn't a mite of breath left in him. I buried him up in the orchard. 'Twasn't my place to take him out to the church burying-ground and spend money for a grave plot. *He wasn't my folks.* I only *married* him. I was trying to get someone to work the land. I was glad when it was all over. I've had better luck hiring—and cheaper. Besides, he spoiled the land.

MARY: I get tired of hearing you talk about the *land,* Marthe. One would think that your land was the only land in the world and that all the rest of the earth was water. You've slaved and dug. And all for the *land.* And your pa and ma slaved and dug and 'twas for the *land.* And what did they get out of it more than a living? And what have you got out of it more than a living?

MARTHE: [*She rises and points to the fields outside the window with a trembling finger. Her voice crackles with anger and passion.*]: I expect you wouldn't know, you and your folks have always had land. Your folks had it in the old country and you've had it here. My pa and ma came over from County Moynihan years back when I was a little thing in arms. They came over steerage with all they had on their backs and a bundle or two besides. In the old country they'd never had land or anything but black poverty and curses. And they came over here—and old Thurman Barnes had the selling of this township and he brought them up here and put them on a bit of wild land where there was an old log shanty the lumberman had left. But it looked like a palace to my ma and pa. And the land. . . . Sure, now, you couldn't find a prettier field than that one beyond the brook; and the wood lot—sure they're fine trees, and there's the swale below the barn. It's a fine place for grass. Well, my pa and ma took the land and they bound over their work for a bit until they could get seed and get started farming. And they prospered and paid for the land. There was a lot to do then—logging and clearing the fields and picking up the stone and raising crops and sheep and cattle. I never had time to learn much except how to work in the fields, and I grew up loving the land just as my ma and pa loved it. We never wanted to leave it. And after a while my pa built this frame house and a frame barn and all the neighbors helped at the "raising"; and he built a cow shed out of the old logs—and the place came on—and we had a living and never saw black poverty this side of the water. [*Standing up and*

154

speaking fiercely] Haven't I wood in my shed, Mary Davis, and pork in my cellar, and a barrel of flour and sugar, and dried cod, and all a body could want? And don't my hens lay my eggs to buy all I'm wanting at the store? And haven't I a good bit laid by? And you say I've had *just a living*. Sure there's many that have had fine and plenty and had no more than I. [*A knocking is heard at the door.*] Who's that? Hide the tea, Mary Davis. I've no mind to be asking the neighbors to eat. Shut the pantry and go the door.

[*She sits down; Mary opens the door. In the doorway with one foot on the sill a young man of about twenty-one is standing. Slightly behind him is a girl perhaps a year or two younger. The boy is olive-skinned with smoothly brushed dark hair and bright dark blue eyes. He has the look of a young eagle. The girl is bareheaded with heavy golden hair half clouding her eyes. Her skin is tanned to a golden shade. They look radiantly happy.*]

MARY: It's only my John—and Lucie.

MARTHE: Your John? Put the tea back on the stove. Will ye come in and sit down and bring the young lady in? We'll have tea and some biscuits that yer gran is going to make and I've a comb of honey on the shelf. Come in.

[*Mary Davis pulls out two of the stiff-backed chairs from their places against the wall and dusts them with her apron. The boy and girl sit down.*]

JOHN: Hello, Gran! Well, aren't you going to speak to Lucie?

MARY: Of course I am! [*Shakes hands*] How do you do, Lucie? I'm glad to see you. How is your mother?

LUCIE: She's very much better.

MARY: You had the new doctor from Warrensburg, didn't you?

LUCIE: Yes, and he gave her something that helped her very much.

MARTHE [*Querulously*]: Mary Davis, why don't you tell me who the young lady is. I don't know her voice. You forget I haven't my eyes. You needn't be thinking I don't *want* to see.

MARY: I'm sorry, Marthe. I thought you knew Lucie. This is Lucie Oliver, our new school teacher.

MARTHE: The one whose folks moved down here out of Canada?

MARY: Yes. She's been teaching over in the Spruce Mountain District and now she's hired out to our trustee and she's going to teach here in this district.

LUCIE [*Rises and comes over to Marthe*]: How do you do, Mrs. Rigney. I'm glad to come and see you.

MARTHE: How de do, how de do. I don't see many young folks. They don't come often to see an old lady, and when they do come, I can't see em plain unless the sun shines right in their faces. Then I can see a little. Won't ye stay and have some biscuits and honey? [*A ray of sunlight from the window lights up Lucie's hair.*] The sun is around your head, Miss Lucie. Lucie—I like that name. And you're teaching school—teaching school. You must know a lot. Be ye John's girl?

JOHN: Now, Mis' Rigney—

MARTHE: Nothing to be ashamed of, is there? You can tell *me*. Be ye courting?

MARY: Marthe Rigney, have you lost your manners? Maybe they *are* courting, but you and I aint. Let them alone.

JOHN [*Holding out a paper bag*]: I came to bring you something, Mis' Rigney . . . oranges. [*He empties the bag into her lap.*] I got them when I was "down below"—in Albany. They're big ones.

MARTHE [*Feeling one*]: I never had such big ones before. Ye got them in Albany?

MARY: Yes, Marthe. John's been down to Albany to work and he's going back next week. He's been offered a good position down there. Did you ever see such oranges?

MARTHE: No, I never did. [*Marthe Rigney lifts one of the oranges until it catches a ray of light and shines like a ball of gold. She lifts it to her nose and sniffs a little.*] Thank ye, thank ye. It's good of ye, John, to remember an old blind woman. I remember the first time I ever set eyes on an orange. My pa was drawn on a jury and he went off to the county seat. And he drove away in the new buggy with our brown mare and it was a fortnight before he came back. And I watched for him every day up the road, and after a while one day I saw the mare come trotting up the valley road, and I hid behind the dooryard gate, but my pa saw me and when he drove past the gate to put the horse up in the barn, he threw me something yellow and round that looked like the moon. And it rolled in the grass and I ran after it and picked it up and ran to show my ma what my pa had brought me. And my ma said it was an orange. I had never seen anything like it before.

LUCIE: Did you like it when you tasted it?

MARTHE: I never tasted an orange for many a day after that. I couldn't bear to cut it or take the peel off; it was so pretty and I kept it in the cupboard and took it out and looked at it every day until it was rotten. And my ma planted the seeds and they came up little smooth green trees with sweet smelling leaves and I thought they would grow but the frost killed them. . . . [*Slowly*] I remember that *first* orange—I thought it was *the moon*.

JOHN: Well, these are not moons and you are to eat them right away and not put them in the cupboard. [*To Lucie*] We must be going, Lucie, if I'm to get down to the post office before six o'clock.

156

MARTHE: Now, John and Miss Lucie, I thought ye were going to stay and have supper with an old blind woman.

LUCIE: Thank you so much. I'd love to stay but John has to get to the post office before it closes. He expects a letter from Albany.

MARTHE: Perhaps you'll go down to Albany with him sometime, eh?

LUCIE: Perhaps—some time.

JOHN [*Taking her arm*]: Perhaps *soon*, Mis' Rigney. Will you come to our wedding? [*To Lucie*] Now don't mind, Lucie. Gran would tell her tomorrow anyway. It's nicer to tell her ourselves.

MARTHE [*At the word "wedding" she rises out of her chair. Her features work with excitement, the wrinkles gathering into knots and then loosening again. The ghost of her youth glooms in her eyes.*]: So ye're courting. I felt it when ye came in. And ye're going to be married soon—a wedding—a wedding. Come here, both of ye. Come close. Don't be afraid of an old blind woman. I want to touch yer faces. I want to see with my hands. [*John and Lucie come close to her and half kneel by her side. The sun catches them all in its dying splendor. Marthe runs her right hand lightly over John's face.*] Why, ye're not a boy any longer—ye're a man grown, John. And I'm not too blind to see that ye're tall and wide at the shoulders and that yer eyes are shining. Miss Lucie, may I touch yer face?

LUCIE: Of course you may. I'm so sorry you don't see well.

MARTHE: Soft and young and yer hair is soft and yer going to have a wedding.

JOHN: There, there. Take it easy, Mis' Rigney. You'll come to our wedding, won't you?

MARTHE [*She does not listen*]: A wedding—soft and young—[*She strokes the hair.*]

LUCIE: There, there, you *will* come, Mis' Rigney, won't you? I'm so happy that I want everybody to come to my wedding and be as happy as I am.

JOHN: Gran, we must go or we'll find the post office closed. We'll stop in on the way back and take you home with us.

MARY: Stop if you see a light. If I've gone home there won't be a light.

JOHN: Goodbye, Mis' Rigney. Goodbye, Gran. [*They go.*]

[*Mary Davis starts for the pantry. Half way there she comes back and opens the doors of the old fashioned stove and puts in two fresh sticks through the griddle in the top. The burned coals make a glow in the room. The sun's light is fading; twilight begins to darken the shadows.*]

MARTHE: I'm thinking I can't eat the biscuits so you've no need to make them. And you needn't cut the comb of honey. I'm not hungry. You can put on a pot of tea and have a cup yourself. But perhaps you'd like biscuits.

MARY [*Startled by Marthe's unwonted solicitude*]: I don't want biscuits and I've honey at home. I'll slick up a bit and make the tea and then I'll go home and get supper for John. He'll be wanting something to eat when he gets back from the post office. And perhaps Lucie'll stop and have a bite with us. I'll make the tea now.

[*Mary lights the kerosene lamp on the shelf and sets it on the plant stand. Then she puts the tea back on the stove and goes into the pantry. She brings two old fashioned blue tea cups without handles and sets them down on the hearth. She takes a blue china sugar bowl from the shelf by the clock and carefully measures a teaspoon of sugar into each cup. She puts the sugar bowl back on the shelf and then puts the tea into the cups. She replaces the pot on the stove and hands Marthe a cup of tea. Then she takes the other and sits down in the rocker with the cup of tea in her lap. The firelight plays on their old faces, giving them the look of sybils.*]

MARTHE: Did ye put the sugar in?

MARY: Yes, I put the sugar in. Why don't you stir your tea?

MARTHE: I went to Albany once—where your John's been. I went as far as Rome. We went up from Albany on the packet boat on the Erie Canal. I remember sitting up on top of the boat all day long in my starched skirts with the green fields sliding past me. I never went anywhere else though.

MARY: That was your own fault if you didn't, Marthe. You've had money to go where you liked, and you had it long before your sight failed. You could a gone anywhere you'd a mind to go—Albany or New York—or even back to the old country; you could a gone.

MARTHE: I could a gone with my feet, Mary, but I couldn't have gone with my head, because my head couldn't see that I ought to go. My eyes were looking always at my bit of land, the cow yard and the pasture and I was seeing that the pasture fence needed mending and thinking what I'd plant in the fallow lot in the spring. Now that I can't see much, I do see that I ought to have gone many places. But now it's too late to go, Mary. I should have gone more places than you know—more than you'll ever know.

MARY: You always were a blow-hard, Marthe. What places could you go that I couldn't know about?

MARTHE: Places I could see in my head in the dark before the lamp was lit. I can see them now in the fire. But I never went to see them—and I never did anything but stay at home and work. I never did anything I should a done. I'm thinking now that I might a married that fine young man, Michael Callahan, when I was young, not waiting until I was forty past to drive a bargain with a hired man to keep him on the

158

land. I might have had a grandson like your John—and his wedding coming on. I might have had a lad to stroke my face when I was young and give me lovin'. I know all I might have had better than you know it. And the land out there took it all from me. Now when I'm sitting alone looking at it I'm thinking if it can give me back smooth cheeks and soft hair and a fine lad and days and nights to be courting together.

MARY: You're in your dotage, Marthe Rigney. You—to be talking of smooth cheeks and loving, at your age.

MARTHE: You don't know my age.

MARY: To be sure I don't—but I can see your face. I'm going home to get supper for John.

MARTHE [*She gets up with sudden energy and screams.*]: And I'm going to *die*.

MARY [*Shaking Marthe by the shoulder*]: Stop blaspheming! You'll die when your time comes—not before, although you're stubborn enough to defy the Almighty and have your own way. You've always had it—ever since you were born.

MARTHE: Help me into the bedroom. I've a queer feeling in here [*puts hand over her heart*] and I tell you I'm going to die. I've found out that there's loving in the world—going on all the time—passing me by. [*She almost screams the last sentence.*]

MARY [*Helping her to the bedroom door*]: The Lord will punish you.

MARTHE [*Pushing her hands off*]: I'm going to die!

MARY [*She comes back leaving the door open*]: I'll come down in the morning.

MARTHE [*Standing in the doorway*]: I'll go to sleep for a while. I'm terribly sleepy. [*In a louder voice*] I'll die when I've a mind to, Mary Davis. [*She disappears in the bedroom.*]

> [*Mary Davis puts wood on the fire, closes the pantry door and hangs her apron on a peg by the pantry door, also her coat which has hung under the hat. She tiptoes to the bedroom door and peers inside. Then she blows out the kerosene lamp and goes.*
> *The glow from the fire lights the room and fills it with flickering shadows. As the fresh wood burns the glow from the hearth becomes brighter. A knock comes at the door. It is repeated. Then the door opens and John and Lucie come in. They are carrying packages and Lucie has a bouquet of late roses and sweet scented pinks.*]

JOHN: Gran's gone home, I guess.

LUCIE: Where's Mrs. Rigney.

JOHN: Look in her bedroom. [*Lucie tiptoes to the door and comes back with her finger to her lips.*] She's asleep. We'll leave the things here for her. Let us put them on the stand and move it up beside her chair. She'll see them first thing in the morning.

[John moves the plant stand up beside the armchair. Lucie unwraps a small jar of bright colored candies and puts it on the stand. She opens another parcel and takes out a white china hen.]

Where are you going to put that?

LUCIE: We'll put it right here beside the candy. She'll like it on account of her hens. Can you get me a vase for the flowers?

JOHN: A vase! A vase in Marthe Rigney's house! She wouldn't know a vase if she saw one. I'll get a tumbler out of the pantry. *[He comes back empty-handed.]* I can't find anything but teacups.

LUCIE: Oh, I know. *[Looks at the clock shelf]* I'll put them in that lovely blue sugar bowl.

JOHN: Will that do? It's full of sugar.

LUCIE: Empty the sugar into a teacup and put some water in it. That's lovely for the flowers. It's awfully old, isn't it? *[Examining it and arranging the flowers]* There—that's pretty. *[Sets them on the plant stand]*

JOHN: But she can't see them.

LUCIE: She can touch them and smell them, can't she? Anyway I'm so happy I wanted to bring her something—a little happiness. Now suppose I were blind *[Closes her eyes]* I would put my hands over the flowers like this—*[Touches them]* and smell them—so—*[Lifts them to her face. John has come behind her. He puts his arm around her and kisses her.]*

JOHN: And—not hear me coming—and I'd kiss you—so—

LUCIE: Sh-h-h. She might wake up.

JOHN: She won't. Besides, she's a little deaf. Lucie! *[Kisses her]*

LUCIE: John!

JOHN *[Holding Lucie in his arms, but a little way apart from him so that he can look at her.]*: Lucie, I can't tell you. I never can tell you. I see your face everywhere I look. I want to come and touch your sleeve or the hem of your skirt, and I want to pick you up and carry you off and tell you things I can't even think about yet. About places we've never been. And yet where it seems we've always been—white water and waves tumbling and great ships—and some place where we've been hundreds of years ago and lived together and died. And a place where there is a great wood. I can see you coming to me out of the wood with the sun shining on your hair.

LUCIE: I know, John, I know. I think those things too. *[She runs her hands over his face, over his lips, neck, arms, sliding them down to his waist.]* I can see with my fingers like old

160

Marthe. I could find you if I were blind. John, don't you ever think you have been someone else—perhaps someone who *was* blind—and loved me when you were that someone else?

JOHN: I've always loved you and I'm frightened for fear of losing you. Why I wake up at night and for a minute I can't remember where you are and I feel that you have gone away—that I've lost you—and I'm nearly crazy. And then I get my senses and know you are alive and that you love me and it's like coming home again after being lost. Say we shall always be together, Lucie. Say it. I can't bear to think of things ever coming to an end.

LUCIE: We shall always be together, John, always—

JOHN: Always.

LUCIE: John, suppose *she* had had a lover when she was young, would he have been like you?

JOHN: No. He would have been an Irish boy—one that came over from County Moynihan where her folks came from—not a bit like me.

LUCIE: What would *he* have said to *her*? I wonder.

JOHN [*Backing towards the door*]: I'll tell you; I've read it in books. [*He swaggers toward her*] He'd say—

LUCIE: Well, what would he say?

JOHN: Well, first tell me what she would say.

LUCIE: That's not hard. I've read a book too. [*She tucks up her skirt in imitation of an Irish colleen and winds her neck scarf about her head. She assumes an Irish accent.*] And it's a great lad ye are to be coming overseas a dazzling a poor girl like me wid yer tongue a saying words that shine like the stars themselves. There's a doubt in me that says I'm dreaming, but if I'm not, why Ill say I knew the first time my eyes fell on ye, that you were the lad I'd be loving. It's you and I will be having great days loving and long nights sitting by the fire.

JOHN [*Assuming a strong Irish accent and swaggering*]: Sure, and it's from far off that I've come to ye, Marthe Rigney, and it's long I've been waiting for this time and searching ye out, Rose o'the World that ye are. And now I've found ye, it's blinded I know I was in my long wandering. For I had not the thought that yer two eyes were like the stars and it's half blinded I am again at the sight of ye and it's many a lad will go envying me the length of his days—And if ye love me, it's I that will be walking humble all me life—knowing it's I that'll be taking the honey of your lips and it's I that would come back to ye from the wild waters of the Seven Seas and the four corners of the earth—and ye might be old, Marthe Rigney, but I always see you young and I'd sing to you always. [*He sings.*]

Pastheen Finn

Love of my heart, my fair Pastheen
Her cheeks are red as the rose's sheen
Like apple blossom her house is white
And her neck is a swan's on a March morn bright.

[*At the beginning of John's speech, Marthe appears in the bedroom door. She clutches the sill and peers out listening. After he sings she leans a bit heaving against the door. It creaks and startles Lucie.*]

LUCIE: Sh-h-h. She's awake. [*Takes John by the arm.*] Come now, we must go. [*They fly out by the woodshed door shutting it softly behind them. They do not see Marthe.*]

[*A pause*]

MARTHE [*In her bewilderment listening to John she believes that Michael Callahan has come back.*]: Michael [*Softly*] Michael [*Again softly*] Michael [*Raising her voice*] have you come back at last. Your voice is still young—young as it was when ye sang that song to me years ago. [*She advances groping with her hand and her cane.*] Michael, I can't be seeing so well now. Where are you. Let me touch your hand—my fingers are my eyes now. Are you bearded, Michael, or smooth. You must let me touch your face. [*The silence begins to sift down heavily.*] Michael [*Poignantly*] why don't you speak? I'll take back all the bitter words now. Something in me wasn't awake, wasn't born when you left me. I think it was my heart. But it's born now, Michael . . . I [*Puts her hand to her heart.*] It hurts me, Michael. It's been hurting a long time. [*A pause. She becomes suspicious.*] Why don't you answer me? Don't be holding anger. We're both too old to be foolish. I've just thought that you were old too, Michael. Someway I always thought you'd never be old . . . like me. [*She creeps out and searches the room with her hands and cane. Her face tells the story of her final realization that the room is empty. She gropes to her arm chair, clutches it and sits down. The light of the fire plays over her face. She feels for the plant stand and finds the china hen. She examines it and puts it back. Then she discovers the flowers. She sinks back in the chair.*] Michael . . . Michael [*Her voice is strange.*] I sent him away . . . Michael, that's a fine name . . . [*She sinks back in her chair holding the flowers.*] I'm tired . . . Michael . . . tired . . . Loving going on all the time . . .

[*The firelight flares up for a moment and in its glow she seems to see her strength is going. She half rises and whispers.*]

Michael.

[*She tries to lift the flowers but collapses and falls back in the chair dead. The light of the fire illumines her face for a moment and then dies down leaving the stage in darkness.*]

CURTAIN

162

NOTES

The following abbreviations are used in the notes:
JRF   Jeanne Robert Foster
LNO   Lucia N. Oliver
RR   Ruth Riedinger
AAR   Albert A. ("Tex") Riedinger
PS   Paul Schaefer
AS   Aline Saarinen
WC   Warder Cadbury
AAA/SI   Archives of American Art, Smithsonian Institution, Washington, D.C.
NYPL   Rare Books and Manuscripts Division (Astor, Lenox and Tilden foundations), The New York Public Library, New York, New York

1. JRF to RR, January 19, 1970.
2. *Warrensburg News,* August 2, 1963, p. 3.
3. LNO to JRF, December 9, 1890.
4. JRF to PS, December 1, 1969.
5. JRF, biographical data, undated.
6. LNO to JRF, June 12, 1896.
7. JRF to PS, December 1, 1969.
8. JRF to RR, March 3, 1962.
9. *Ibid.,* December 25, 1960.
10. JRF to AS, December 22, 1959 (Saarinen Papers, AAA/SI).
11. JRF to Winifred LaRose, May 28, 1970.

May I congratulate you on finding an almost perfect "Harrison Fisher Book." The *Cup of Tea* is the only "Harrison Fisher Book[.]" As the pages are not numbered and I do not wish to sully the book even with pencil marks I will set down—from Fisher's titles the ones for which I posed. Sometimes they do not resemble me—as the Jane Cable illustrations for the novel. Jane was described as being a dark brunette so Harrison had to make me a "dark brunette."

The drawing that Harrison considered *my portrait* is the one at the dressing table entitled "Which?" The gown was beautiful, pale lavender and cream lace. At that time I had hip length bronze gold hair. [Following is Jeanne Robert Foster's list of the illustrations from Fisher's *The Cup of Tea* for which she posed.]

> *Which*
> *Rivals*—the blonde
> *A Modern Eve*

The Shifting Sands
A Winter Promenade
Nancy
Jane Cable
In Clover
Taking Toll
Not Yet but Soon
Gathering Honey
Jane Cable and Graydon
Four Studies of Jane Cable (the one called Nedra-portrait)
You Will Marry a Dark Man
The Summer Girl
Illustration from Schribners

Of course he did many more of me that appeared in various magazines and particularly in the Hearst newspapers. I have many of the newspapers but only one copy and that about to fall apart.

My largest list was from the pencil of Albert Wenzell. I also posed for Charles Dana Gibson and in Paris for "PAL" the great color photographer. In New York we belonged to the Model's Club. There was no roystering. We all worked. Many times we could—in small ways—help the artists and they invariably were friendly, courteous and kind.

12. JRF to AS, December 22, 1959 (Saarinen Papers, AAA/SI).
13. JRF to RR, December 25,1960.
14. It is difficult to verify the date of JRF's move to Boston. For one thing, she began to make certain "adjustments" to her age. JRF began to list the year of her birth as 1884, rather than 1879, as early as 1922, when it appeared in *Who's Who in America* (Chicago: A. N. Marquis and Company, 1922–23), XII, p. 1152.
15. JRF to Dr. Harold Martin, President of Union College, Schenectady, N.Y., September 9, 1965.
16. JRF to RR, January 27, 1967.
17. William James to Henry Whitman, Springfield Center, N.Y., June 16, 1895, cited by Paul Jamieson, ed., *Adirondack Reader* (2d. ed.; Glens Falls, N.Y.: The Adirondack Mountain Club, Inc., 1982), p. 110.
18. JRF to PS, December 1, 1969.
19. Philip G. Terrie, *Forever Wild: Environmental Aesthetics and the Adirondack Forest Preserve* (Philadelphia: Temple University Press, 1985), p. 52.
20. *Ibid.*, p. 4.
21. JRF to PS, December 1, 1969.
22. JRF to AAR, October 6, 1966.
23. Reprinted with permission of Darwin and Jeanne Shaw.
24. LNO to JRF, June 12, 1896.
25. Phyllis C. Robinson, *Willa: The Life of Willa Cather* (New York: Holt, Rinehart and Winston, 1983), pp. 155–60.
26. JRF, biographical data, undated.
27. JRF, biographical data, undated.
28. Joseph Hone (ed.) *J. B. Yeats, Letters to His Son, W. B. Yeats and Others, 1869–1922* (New York: E. P. Dutton and Company, Inc., 1946), p. 180.
29. Albert Shaw, Jr., to Noel Riedinger, July 19, 1969.
30. JRF to Mary Conroy Anderson, June 4, 1960 (Foster-Murphy Collection, NYPL).
31. *Ibid.*
32. Hone, ed., *Yeats, Letters to His Son*, p. 180.
33. Ezra Pound to John Quinn, February 21, 1922 (John Quinn Memorial Collection, NYPL).
34. Interview with Judith Fetterley, February 12, 1986.
35. JRF to Mary Conroy Anderson, June 4, 1960 (Foster-Murphy Collection, NYPL).
36. JRF to AS, February 22, 1960 (Saarinen Papers, AAA/SI).
37. *Portland* (Me.) *Sunday Telegraph,* May 11, 1930.
38. JRF, biographical data, undated.
39. Judith Zilczer, *"The Noble Buyer:" John Quinn, Patron of the Avant-Garde* (Washington: Smithsonian Institution Press, 1978), p. 47.
40. Bernard J. Poli, *Ford Madox Ford and the transatlantic review* (Syracuse, N.Y.: Syracuse University Press, 1967), pp. 163–65.

41. JRF, biographical data, undated.

42. Alfred Kazin, *An American Procession* (New York: Alfred A. Knopf, 1984), p. 334.

43. John Quinn to Ezra Pound, December 12, 1921 (John Quinn Memorial Collection, NYPL).

44. JRF to PS, December 6, 1969.

45. Judith Zilczer, *"The Noble Buyer,"* pp. 9–10.

46. *Ibid.*

47. JRF to C[l]ara Oliver Smith (sister), May 1, 1932.

48. JRF to WC, February 24, 1958.

49. JRF, from lecture notes on municipal housing, undated.

50. JRF, biographical data, undated; JRF to AAR and RR, undated; JRF to PS, March 21, 1970.

51. *A Decent Home,* printed by the Schenectady Muncipal Housing Authority, 1959, p. 1.

52. *Ibid.,* p. 17.

53. *Ibid.*

54. Interview with Joseph Mosarra, retired executive director of Schenectady Senior Citizens Center, November 8, 1984.

55. References to JRF appear in the following publications: Bernard J. Poli, *Ford Madox Ford and the transatlantic review* (Syracuse, N. Y.: Syracuse University Press, 1967); B. L. Reid, *The Man from New York: John Quinn and His Friends* (New York: Oxford University Press, 1968); Michael Holroyd, *Augustus John* (New York: Holt, Rinehart and Winston, 1974); William M. Murphy, *Prodigal Father: The Life of John Butler Yeats* (Ithaca, N.Y.: Cornell University Press, 1978); Judith Zilczer, *"The Noble Buyer": John Quinn, Patron of the Avant-Garde* (Washington: Smithsonian Institution Press, 1978); Harriet Zinnes, ed., *Ezra Pound and the Visual Arts* (New York: New Directions Publishing Corp., 1980); Betsy G. Fryberger, *Gwen John* (Stanford, Calif.: Stanford University Museum of Art, 1982). References to her were included in Ford Madox Ford, *It Was the Nightingale* (Philadelphia: J. B. Lippincott Company, 1933), and Joseph Hone, ed., *J. B. Yeats: Letters to His Son W. B. Yeats and Others, 1869–1922* (New York: E. P. Dutton and Company, Inc., 1946).

56. JRF to PS, March 21, 1970.

57. Terrie, *Forever Wild,* pp. 8, 148–49.

58. *Ibid.*

59. From notes by Jeanne Robert Foster, July 3, 1967:

> My mother was adopted—but not legally—by Enos Putnam, the elder and Sybil Daly Putnam, his wife, Wesleyans. Enos Putnam and the neighbors built the old Johnsburg Church in 1859. They lived originally in a log house near the church on the Mill Creek Road, now called Garnet Lake Road.
>
> This Enos Putnam was a friend of Nathan Davis—always called Nate—of Johnsburg, and his daughter Frances Davis was the intimate and dearest friend of my mother. Since the Putnams and the Davis family had a better education than the other members of the community, they naturally spent much time together.
>
> Although my mother moved away into Essex County when I was two years old, I spent much time in Johnsburg summers, and my mother's stories of Nate Davis, his books, his telescope, his genius, were often told to me.
>
> In Johnsburg, even when I was growing up, he was always referred to by other families as "the astronomer." He wrote a pamphlet, "Natural Science and the Solar System."

60. Many of the photograph captions contain general information about the Adirondacks. This information can be found in the following:

> Jane Eblen Keller, *Adirondack Wilderness: A Story of Man and Nature* (Syracuse, N. Y.: Syracuse University Press, 1980), Frank Graham, Jr., *The Adirondack Park, A Political History* (New York: Alfred A. Knopf, 1978, paperback rpt. Syracuse, N.Y.: Syracuse University Press, 1985), Harold Hochschild, *Township 34* (privately printed, 1952), Lincoln Barnett, *The Ancient Adirondacks* (New York: Time-Life Books, 1974), as well as in many other excellent books about the Adirondacks.

61. Interview with Mabel Jones, Historian, Town of Minerva, March 19, 1984.

62. *Minerva: A History of a Town in Essex County* (Minerva, N.Y.: Minerva Historical Society, 1967), pp. 54, 69.

63. JRF to Helen Shevlin, December 11, 1967.

64. Interview with Mabel Jones and Helen Shevlin, April 10, 1984.

65. JRF, unfinished poems, "Sybil" and "Bedquilts."

66. *Minerva: A History of a Town in Essex County,* pp. 164–65.

67. JRF, unfinished poems, "Sybil" and "Bedquilts."

68. *Minerva: A History of a Town in Essex County,* pp. 164–65.

69. "'My First Journey' written by Jean E. Foster, English, December 1909" was on the original work. JRF used many names—Jean, Julie, Jeanne—during her lifetime.

70. Interview with Thomas and Jane Parrott, Historians, Town of Chester, April 4, 1984.

71. JRF to AAR, December 6, 1966.

72. JRF to Sara Bowyer O'Conner, October 6, 1962:

> First something about the Braley house. It was called the Revolutionary House because it stood there during the Revolution. When we moved into the house the vents for guns in the long loft-attic had not been closed. The small barn was built by my father. What we know of the house was this: The Braley family owned it for a *very* long time. "Rilly" Braley was the mother of Mrs. Fernando Gould. When Fernando built the house—a little farther up on the right-hand side of Main St.—and the widowed "Rilly" was left alone, she moved in with her daughter and rented the old house. When we lived there, one had to step *down* to enter the bedrooms and the pantry and the summer kitchen; the old beams were in the corners of the rooms and the inside of the front porch was lathe and plastered—very quaint. I mentioned the room with the worn floorboards. We used it for storage, for it was the room that had had an iron grill made by the local blacksmith to confine "the dancing man" who danced himself to death. Mother would hardly enter the room.

73. *History of Warren County* (Glens Falls, N.Y.: Board of Supervisors of Warren County, 1963), pp. 196–197.

74. *Warrensburg News,* August 2, 1963.

75. *Ibid.*

76. JRF to PS, December 1, 1969.

77. JRF to RR, February 6, 1970; JRF, explanatory data, 1969.

78. Interview with Myrtle Putnam Buyce, June 30, 1984.

79. Interview with Adeline Armstrong O'Byrne, January 26, 1985.

80. *Minerva: A History of a Town in Essex County,* p. 53.

81. Interview with Adeline Armstrong O'Byrne, January 26, 1985.

82. Interview with Mabel Jones, March 19, 1984.

83. Hochschild, *Township 34,* p. 267.

84. JRF to RR, February 6, 1970; JRF, explanatory data, 1969.

85. JRF to Sara Bowyer O'Conner, October 6, 1962:

> Lucia Newell, my mother, was adopted five times before she was adopted by the Putnams [later renamed Eliza Putnam]. My grandfather, William Newell, a lumberman and raftsman, was drowned in the Hudson at North River about 1860. His only marker is a white birch tree almost across from the old North River Hotel. Lucinda Weller Newell, his wife, stood on the bank with her four little girls and saw him lose hold on a rock and wave goodbye. The girls were Hattie, Elizabeth, Lucia (my mother), and Nancy.

> JRF to WC, June 27, 1961:

> In regard to the old river drivers my grandfather William Newell was a shanty man and river driver, and he was drowned at North River five miles above North Creek where the river widens out before it pours into a gorge-like channel. He lies beside the river, the only marker a white birch tree, now very old. I am the only grandchild who went back to the river, found the spot and sketched it in watercolor. Sometimes I feel that his spirit moves in my veins.

86. JRF to RR, February 6, 1970; JRF, explanatory data, 1969.

87. JRF to WC, February 24, 1958.

88. JRF, *Neighbors of Yesterday* (Boston: Sherman, French and Co., 1916; reprinted Schenectady, N.Y.: Riedinger and Riedinger Ltd.), inserted between pp. 90–91, (R&R edition).

89. JRF to RR, January 19, 1970.

90. JRF to PS, October 11, 1969.

INDEX

(Page references in italics indicate photographs or illustrations.)